Ridin'  Jumpin' Over Cars

The Biography of Virginia Reger

A True Rodeo Star

Elaine Smith

Virginia Reger

Ridin' Ropin' & Jumpin' Over Cars
The Biography of Virginia Reger—A True Rodeo Star
Copyright 2017 Blazing Star Books

ALL RIGHTS RESERVED

No part of this publication may be reproduced, stored in a retrieval system or transmitted in any form or by any means — electronic, mechanical, photocopying, recording or otherwise without prior written permission from Blazing Star Books.

Cover design by Blazing Star Books

For information about this or other titles visit

www.blazingstarbooks.com

ISBN: 978-1546885634

Virginia Reger has led an amazing life. Now leaning toward 90 years young, her story is told through the memorabilia she saved over the years and the recorded memories sparked by those images.

This biography is meant to serve as an example for women and girls showing what drive, determination, and persistence can accomplish. Though her body may be weaker, her mind is strong and she will continue to share her stories. Here we present that little gal who went far in

Ridin' Ropin' & Jumpin' Over Cars

The Early Days

Virginia's first memory of attending a rodeo is the fancy costumes the women performers wore. Blouses of satin and lace, wool pants, and felt cowboy hats appeared to the four year old girl to be the uniform of the rich and famous. The Great Depression overshadowed many aspects of life, yet these women seemed to be immune to the poverty gripping the country. Living in rural Oklahoma on a large ranch, the Regers were never hungry. But Virginia wanted one of those satin blouses. And if it took becoming a rodeo performer to have one, that's what she would do. And that is exactly what Virginia Reger did.

When she was just a toddler, grandfather Crouch sat the girl unsteadily on the back of one of his tamest plow horses. She promptly fell off and onto the dusty ground. An immediate and loud cry brought Opal Reger running toward her sobbing baby daughter. But Grandpa Crouch picked little Virginia up, dusted her off, and stopped his daughter from interfering by saying, "Oh, she just wants to get back on. Then she'll quit cryin'." He sat the ten-month-old back on the horse and, sure enough, her tears dried and she loved it. That moment defined the direction her life would take for many years to come.

Monte Reger, her father, chose an unusual animal from a herd he and father-in-law George Crouch owned and trained that steer to be a performer.

When Monte was a boy, the only thing his folks could do about his asthma was to send him out west to a dryer climate. It was there he found his calling—he was a cowboy. He loved working the cows and farming the land for George Crouch, who ran a big ranch and farm near Buffalo, OK. Monte didn't tell anybody about his illness and hid it really well. Through competitions with other hands in roping and breaking horses, he developed a taste for rodeo and became a top hand. In 1924, the cowboy married his boss' daughter, Opal, leased some acreage, and continued to farm Crouch's 1700 acres. He was quite good with a rope and, in his words was "feeling pretty salty." Things were looking good for Monte Reger.

He decided putting on a rodeo could be a profitable endeavor and called on some folks in the business to help. In 1925, he helped put on the first rodeo ever held at Doby Springs, OK, and that event reigned supreme for many years to come. Model T Fords, parked bumper-to-bumper, outlined the arena and wagons were arranged to create chutes. Receipts didn't offset the cost, but the rodeo bug bit Monte hard.

Knowing just about everything about cowboying and the emerging rodeo scene, he naturally fell into the announcing position. Way before microphones were available, he used a megaphone. But during the week, his job was plowing and planting fields of wheat. He was quoted in a story from 1980 in The Quarter Horse Journal, "…you know, you get ideas to do something better. When a man is sitting out there on an old gang plow hooked to six or eight head of mules going around a section (660 acres) of land, he has a lot of time to think. I got to figuring one day that if a person ever got anywhere, he would have to do something different from the ordinary."

It was then he found what would set him apart from the average rodeo performer. That Brahman-Longhorn cross steer was with cattle out of Louisiana. The animals were wild and "rank." Crouch thought it would make good roasts and steaks, but Monte saw his potential. He put the animal in the rodeo as roping steer, though he quickly graduated to the bucking chute and became known as Bobcat Twister. The steer would throw his head and those long and tall horns knocked off every rider who tried to stay on him for eight seconds. Many riders said getting hit with those horns was like somebody smacking you with a two-by-four.

When the steer was seven years old, Monte had the idea to tame the animal to use those massive horns as an attraction. He tried lots of techniques and food without much luck, but happened on the treat which would make Bobby happy to perform whatever tricks were asked of him. One day Opal was near the corral throwing out some overcooked, hardened biscuits to the birds. Monte thought he'd see if Bobby might like one. Sure enough, the steer loved them. Bobby would do anything for one of Opals biscuits. Almost.

Once Bobby refused to perform his tricks. Opal made a show of taking the biscuits back to the house and then didn't give him any for several days. When they thought the animal was ready, she stood on the far side of the car with a batch of biscuits and Bobby quickly decided he'd go after them. After that, training was a snap and Opal kept Monte stocked with hard biscuits. It took months, but finally Bobby was ready to perform on the road. Monte's son, Buddy, was getting good at being a rodeo clown and doing an act on a trained miniature mule, so Monte packed up his wife and kids and they took off from Buffalo, Oklahoma to Pennsylvania.

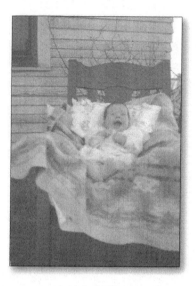

Virginia as a baby. She still has this blanket!

Even at four years old Virginia was strong willed. Insisting to wear her new hat and coat for the photograph, she refused to take it off despite all efforts by Opal and the photographer.

On one trip, Monte decided to go on the road with Bobby and Opal, but would leave the children, now three, at home with the grandparents. Virginia was devastated. She remembers crying and crying while sitting on someone's lap, refusing to believe her parents went on a rodeo adventure without her. But, as children do, she adjusted and even found ways to have fun. Often children from big towns would visit the Crouch ranch and the Reger kids helped with the field trips. Occasionally they would play pranks on the unsuspecting city kids and get a big laugh. But such antics had to be done out of Grandpa Crouch's sight, or they would surely get in big trouble.

While on the road, Opal and Monte found they, too, were unhappy and vowed to travel with the whole family. He built living quarters on the back of a truck and fashioned his own style of motor home. Such vehicles existed, but Monte engineered the Reger camping truck to their own needs. There were bunk beds, a stove, and a trailer hitch. Bobby was loaded in a trailer hooked behind the truck and off they went.

The Reger kids were raised on a ranch with a rope in their hands. But Virginia was a girl and would only be in "play clothes" if no cameras were around. Dresses were reserved for Sunday School. After being on the road with her parents, a quiet time at home was welcomed. School work was most often done through the Calvert correspondence school, but Virginia attended first grade in California while Monte was working with the film industry and doing promotions with Bobby.

A natural born showman, Monte quickly learned how to get attention.

Bobby

The first bovine ever trained to jump over an automobile.

▼

High School Act
Performing Tricks Any Horse Can Do.

▼

Feature Attraction
Madison Square Garden
New York City
and Every State in the Union

▼

An Act that is the Greatest Box Office Drawing Card, Ballyho and Attraction ever Presented to the Public.

▼

Plenty of Flash and Color
Excellent Wardrobe
Two Cars and Trailers
Four Head of Stock
Six People

You have seen him in the movies ~ Let the public see him at your celebration

UP AND OVER

ON WITH THE PARADE

A pamphlet, originally printed in red ink to get attention, featured Bobby, and Opal astride the trailed mule on the front.

But with the grip of the Great Depression strangling the average American, the going was rough. Monte declared in the July 1970 "Quarter Horse Journal" article, "People had never seen anything in their lives like ol' Bobby Twister, but we liked to starved to death. They didn't want to turn loose of those nickels." Opal said the kids never missed a meal, but they ate a lot of hot cakes and beans. And Monte confessed that a lot of farmers wondered how their cows got milked.

The children sold postcards of Bobby at every opportunity. Monte said at four years old, Virginia was "a cute little thing and would say 'mister don't you want to buy a picture?' The only way she'd get turned down was if they did not have any money." She wouldn't give up easily. That was a trait which often appeared throughout her child and adulthood. Another was the panache which drove the girl to become a successful performer.

The kids posed on Bobby, but learned to ride on Grandpa Crouch's big, gray horse named Sparky. They also had chores, one of which was to polish the brass tips on Bobby's horns. Monte would remove them for the kids to work on, but occasionally he polished them in place.

ONE OF THE LAST LONGHORNS. Mr. and Mrs. Monte Reger of Buffalo, Okla., are at the stock show with Bob, trained Texas longhorn steer, one of the last of his breed. The horns are 8 feet 6 inches from tip to tip around the curve.

After the sale of a few postcards, the family would gather up enough money for five gallons of gas and travel down the road till they ran out of gas again. While sitting and waiting on customers, Monte had another flash of inspiration. He bought a dime's worth of orange and nickel's worth of black paint. On the back side of a canvas sign made before they left Oklahoma, he painted, "Feet Like a Cow. Body Like a Moose. Head Like a Deer and Horns Like a? What Monte stirred up was curiosity. Folks paid to find out what that thing in the trailer actually was. Suddenly, they were doing well. They followed the fall fairs through Kansas and realized "Bobby Twister" could draw in the crowds and make a good living for them.

When winter rolled around, Monte worked seriously with Bobby for hours at a time. The strong willed steer resisted learning for a time, but eventually got the idea if he cooperated, Monte would be happy and treat him well. He stopped throwing his head back to knock off the rider. "It felt like someone had hit me with a pole-ax," Monte was quoted saying.

By the end of the winter the steer was pulling a two-wheeled cart, kneeling with Monte on his back, and even jumping over a car. That activity was apparently fun for the steer, as he had been jumping over gates, fences, or vehicles for most of his life. He was a natural, and Monte channeled that talent into an act he could market anywhere. The pair made an appearance at the Johnny Lee Wills Stampede with resounding success. Monte Reger and his "World Famous Educated High Jumping Longhorn Steer" received bookings across the south central United States. He developed his signature move, the "Tip Your Hat." They were so popular; a promoter said he could get Monte all the work he wanted in Vaudeville shows.

However, having "The Largest Horn Steer Alive" on an indoor stage proved problematic. Monte made sure not to feed him prior to a show, but on one occasion Bobby completed his act, knelt down to take a bow, and, in Monte's words, "About then I heard it happen; I looked back and he had sure messed up that clean stage." The showman was horrified and he prepared to make a quick exit. But, "About that time one of the clowns came running out, scooped up that pile and hollered 'hey cowboy you left part of your bull!'" From then on, if it happened, they took advantage of it and got a laugh from the audience.

In 1934, Monte got a contract with Universal Studios to do appearances and promotions at theaters all across the west coast. While in California, Monte and Bobby appeared in a movie. Ken Maynard was a famous cowboy actor and starred in several "Wheels of" movies. Monte was on set as a trapper to help handle Bobby in the unusual situation. Monte Reger had the show business bug, and it spread to his children; especially Virginia. She had just started school, but knew she wanted to be a rodeo performer.

Ken Maynard, the famous cowboy actor, mounted on Bobcat Twister. Monte Reger, below, made his one and only film appearance in "Wheels of Destiny" as "Trapper.

While in California, the Regers had a family photo taken. Virginia sighed when she saw this picture saying, "I look so sad." But she wasn't sad at all. That's her on the far left.

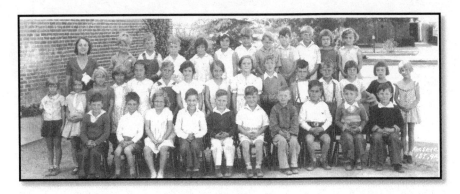

Virginia attended first grade at Roosevelt Grade School in 1933.

An unparalleled businessman and promoter, Monte Reger had his own contract drawn up and duplicated to be absolutely sure of what was expected on both ends of the agreement. The cartoon was drawn by the famous Robert Ripley, most known for creating Ripley's Believe It or Not, which appeared in newspapers all over the USA making Bobby instantly recognizable. The article with the drawing states Bobby travelled over 60,000 miles and jumped automobiles hundreds of times without ever touching one of the vehicles with a hoof. The party of the second part in the contract was not going to let the party of the first part take advantage of him!

While Monte was making appearances in the Los Angeles area such as promoting a sandwich shop and having Bobby box the 1898-1905 heavy weight champion of the world.

On several occasions, Bobby would jump over a table with people pretending to have dinner. At right Monte rides as Bobby clears a checked covered table where famous lady trick riders Mabel Strickland and Paris Williams sit by calmly drinking coffee with delighted smiles on their faces.

This program from October 28, 1934 states in Event No. 9 Bobby, the World's Famous Educated Steer, would be appearing at Madison Square Garden. Monte had indeed made it to the bigtime. And Virginia first saw the "Garden" at age seven.

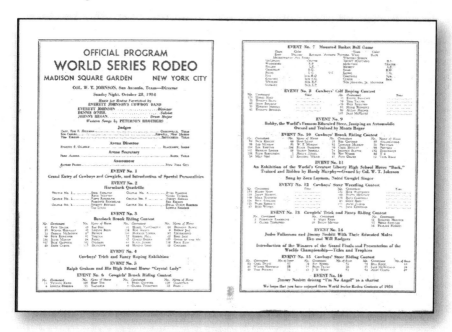

It's not often one would see a man riding a massive horned steer which stood on a trailer pulled by a team of horses. But such sights were common when Monte Reger was in the parade!

Learning the Ropes

When the Regers hooked up with Colonel Jim Eskew and his wife Dolly to announce and perform in the JE Ranch Rodeo, the kids got their chance. Jim Eskew, Jr taught all three children how to rope and trick ride. He was a World Champion Trick Roper and showed them all his tricks.

The little girl had the run of the rodeo and loved to watch the ladies trick roping and riding. She admired their flashy costumes and skill with horses. She again voiced the desire for one of those pretty satin blouses. Her wise mother advised her seven year old daughter that she would have to be a trick rider to have clothes like that. Virginia knew then what she wanted to do. She would become a rodeo performer.

While in the North East United States, the Regers were invited to spend a week with another rodeo family at a lake. Virginia remembers it being a "blast." Opal was appalled a photo was taken of her with bare legs. They took the ponies and swam with them in the lake.

Upon their return to Oklahoma, Grandpa Crouch was shocked to hear Virginia speaking with a New England accent, but it wasn't long before she regained the Oklahoma drawl.

The photo below is not that grandfather, but is another ancestor. This photo was found in a box of memorabilia from Opal's sister, Twila, who took care of the Reger kids when Monte and Opal would travel alone. Eighty-nine year old Virginia held this photo in her hands and said, "He looks like he'd be fun to be around." It is unusual to find a photo of that era, this one is from 1903, in which the subject looks happy. The back of the frame has a handwritten message: "Grandpa Marten went to Cal. during gold rush with team of oxen, 2 other men, gone 2 yrs. 1903 taken. Amy Crouch gfather." Amy was Opal's mother. This is Virginia's great-great grandfather.

While the family travelled with the Wild West Shows, often they would see Buck Owens, who would become a famous country singer and star of the 1970 television show, "Hee Haw." During the 1930's, he was a poor performer but had one sponsor: Baby Ruth candy bars. He had boxes of Baby Ruths and often gave them out to Virginia and the other kids. He admitted occasionally the candy bar was his only source of food. "He was real nice," she remembers.

Below, the whole family stands near a tent set up for the shows.

The Regers met many interesting people on the rodeo circuit. Above is Curly McCall, an employee of Colonel Jim's who carried out many duties quietly and behind the scenes. He didn't consider himself a horseman, yet it was he who rode the famous "Patches" bareback and with no hands while they jumped over the hood of a vehicle. He performed this act regularly, then went back to his more mundane responsibilities.

Below is a postcard found in one of Virginia's scrapbooks of "Chief Winnesheik's Indian Band" which toured with the JE Ranch company. Very colorful characters, Virginia remembers them as very pleasant people.

The Reger Eskew partnership transformed Virginia's life. Eskew, called Colonel out of respect of his tall stature and commanding authority, was known for bringing rodeo to the eastern part of the United States. The native Texas rancher who found a home in upstate New York had quite an operation, with herds of stock and an employee payroll of $1200 per week which is over $20,000 in today's money. He was an expert horseman and well known cowboy. In the 1920's, he worked in Wild West Shows and circuses, and eventually created his own show which toured New England and the Mid-Atlantic states. It was during that time the Regers joined the travelling show.

The rodeo giant hired Monte to be his announcer along with his "Educated Steer" act. Eskew was among the first in the business to feature trick and celebrity acts, knowing the daring moves of trick riders and glamorous movie stars would bring in customers. He was right; the show was a huge success.

When Bobby jumped over the car, Monte would toss the lunge line strap into the air. The steer was loose and the crowd would gasp thinking the impressive animal was out of control. But one spoken command from Monte and Bobby walked calmly to Opal,. She led him back to their area while Monte rushed back up to the announcer's stand.

Jim Eskew, Jr., then about seventeen and shown on the next page, had already made a name for himself as an outstanding trick rider and roper. He rode, roped and performed with the best of the time. The young man took a liking to Monte and his family, and saw their potential as performers. He spent many hours with the Reger kids teaching them riding and roping tricks. One of his more daring performances included skipping rope while riding a horse. He won numerous world championships even into his forties.

Colonel Jim's wife, Dolly Eskew was also a major figure in the rodeo scene. Beautiful, glamorous, she always dressed "to the nines" with satin blouses and lace trims. "Miss Dolly," as everyone called her, taught by example. She, too, was a skilled trick rider and roper having performed in circuses and Wild West shows. Her grace, demeanor, and delightful personality impressed little Virginia, then about seven years old. It was even rumored the woman had appeared as the famed "Prairie Rose," a legendary woman performer in Wild West shows and early rodeo. Miss Dolly's influence is seen in many of the costume designs Virginia created during her career. The woman was almost bigger than life. This added to her mystique.

AMONG THE many stars to participate in the second annual Rodeo show, opening tonight at Houlihan's Circus lot, Menands, is Dolly Askew, noted Texas Rodeo horsewoman, pictured above, on her favorite mount, "Captain."

Junior Eskew taught Virginia many of the rope and riding tricks. He was one of the top performers of the time.

JE Ranch Rodeo was the biggest rodeo company in the East. A native Texan, Eskew found a home in Waverly, NY.

Colonel Jim Eskew was a major player in the rodeo scene during the 1930's and 40's. After he hired the Regers, Virginia had the opportunity to learn the tricks of the trade of performing in the rodeo. He was highly respected and a good leader. The Regers worked with him for much of Virginia's childhood.

On the road in the Reger's homebuilt motor home. Taking advantage of every opportunity for promotion, Monte put the Reger name on every vehicle they used.

Monte taught his kids to "Tip Your Hat" to help them communicate their thanks to the audience reaction and to stand out from the other performers.. It was his signature move.

In Pittsburg, PA, the Regers rode for the Children's Home there. Also, a movie premier was happening and Monte got a special invitation. Drawn by famous artist, Pete Martinez, the card was to be presented at Duquense Garden for the whole family to see the film, "The Man of Conquest." Virginia remembers it being different from the average "Saturday Westerns" she saw while her mother or grandmother was doing the grocery shopping in town back home. It was the story of Sam Houston, the first president of The Republic of Texas and a hero of the Texas revolution against Mexico in 1836. The film was nominated for three academy awards in 1939. But it didn't measure to the "Saturday Westerns Virginia loved.

Monte and Bobby were used as "draws" in the JE Ranch Wild West Rodeo. The sport was just transitioning from Wild West Shows and Vaudeville to include both rodeo competitions and contract performance acts. This article from 1936 declares the steer to be the Longest Horned Steer in the World. That might have been a stretch, but proving otherwise would be difficult. But theirs was a distinctive act with truly unique characters.

Having been taught by her mother and Miss Dolly to always be ready for a photograph opportunity, Virginia dressed in her best costume and practiced roping in front of their trailer. A beautiful, dark haired woman with a perfect, fair complexion approached the little girl and started asking questions. Naturally, she answered eagerly. Virginia didn't know they were in a part of Maine where French was still widely spoken. She talked to the reporter from the French newspaper *Le messager* for a long time and posed for a photograph. In fact, she talked so much, Monte later teased that he thought she would never shut up! None of the Regers had any idea the article would be printed in a French newspaper. That brought customers to the rodeo making Colonel Eskew and the owner of the local rodeo very happy. Eskew made a point to tell the little girl she had done well getting in the paper at such a young age. Little Virginia felt ten feet tall and learned a valuable lesson: always be ready to talk to the press no matter what language they speak, and always look nice when you're out in public.

1936 8 years

Hoop-la!

Voici mesdames et messieurs, une jolie petite "cow-girl" qui fait ses petits trucs tous les soirs sur le terrain de l'Exposition, rue Main. Elle se nomme Virgin*i* Reger et elle est âgée de 7 ans seulement. La voici posée sur le vif s'amusant avec son lasso. E* elle est très habile aussi sur l dos de son petit cheval

Meet the Reger Family—At Home on the Range!

The range in this case is the Tri-City Stadium in Union, where Col. Eskew's Rodeo features stunt riding, roping and broncho-busting tonight and tomorrow night. Louis Feinseth, local attorney, sponsors the show, not the least part of which is played by this family group. From left to right are the daddy, Monte Reger; Buddy, ten; on his favorite mule, "Singer;" Virginia, eight, astride "Speck;" and little Dixie Lee, five, riding "Pal." Opal Reger, at right, is proud mama. (See Much Ado! Page 13)

When the family was travelling, they often were posed together for photos by newspaper photographers who were sent to the rodeo arena. Occasionally, those newspaper people knew nothing of rodeo, livestock, or horses. Virginia couldn't believe some the poses they were asked to do, but her training kept her quiet and she tried her best to cooperate with the photographers.

This is one of the more normal poses, except it was taken after the rodeo and most of their gear was already packed in the car. They had to rush around and Virginia isn't wearing her hat and Buddy tipping his instead of Monte doing his usual routine. The photographer wanted the whole family, but the kids were tired and not all that keen on taking yet another photo. But they kept at it and got their picture in the paper.

MIDDLETOWN TIMES HERALD, MIDDLETOWN, N. Y., TUESDAY, AUGUST 15, 1939.

Rodeo Girls Give 4,000 Children a Thrill

These girls provided many thrills for the 4,000 boys and girls who were entertained at a Pony Day program in Harry Clay Oval by the Orange County Fair Society. They are members of the JE Ranch Rodeo for which their father is announcer. Virginia, eleven, and Dixie, eight, did trick riding on fast-riding ponies. They appear in the evening show also.—Photo by Dougherty.

Events other than the actual rodeo performance were almost always included as promotional opportunities. On August 15, 1939, Virginia demonstrated trick riding done by a young kid before 4000 local children from the Orange County, New York area. The site of the "Pony Day program" mentioned in the photo caption was built as a horse racing track in 1857. Around 1920 it was converted to a dirt track for racing cars and named the "Harry Clay Oval." At the time of this photo, Tri-City Arena in Union, NJ was a race track and fairground which often hosted rodeos and circuses. Virginia remembers seeing and hearing race cars which would run during the day, then the rodeo would set up their pens and fences for the evening. Buggy races with trotting horses (which were faster than most running horses) were also held. The bowl of the arena was depressed into the earth, and after it fell out of use became a dump ground. In the 1950's, a bowling alley was built there. Imagine, future archeologists might find horse shoes, cowboy boots, and bowling shoes in the same place.

There were many child performers in the Wild West Shows and Rodeos. Virginia, here on the second row third from the right, achieved one of her dreams at this young age. She wears a satin blouse made by Opal and a felt hat, feeling like a grown up among the kids. A fan made white vests with red trim and a bow for her hair. Seen here with flowers in her hair, this was taken after a trick riding performance. Flowers stay put where hats come off when one is upside down. Other kids in the photo were also trick riders and ropers. The Native American children danced with their parents and stayed in tents fashioned to appear as teepees. Virginia remembers most of the children were very nice, though some were spoiled and rather difficult.

Here among the cowgirls employed by the J. E. Ranch Rodeo, Virginia stands at the far left of the front row. This was one of the postcards sold by the rodeo company and the photographer was the famous Ralph Doubleday, who is considered the first and undisputed champion rodeo photographer. Notice Miss Dolly there on the back row.

Ralph R. Doubleday was a legendary photographer. He specialized in rodeo action shots and often risked being injured to get just the right shot. Cameras were bulky and inconvenient, yet Doubleday excelled in getting excellent photographs of both still models and action packed movement.

This is a signed portrait given to Virginia during one of their photo shoots. He often photographed her. She remembers him as a quiet, nice man. He was inducted into the National Cowboy Hall of Fame in 1958, credited with over 4000 photographs dated from 1910 to 1955.

Herbert Maddy, a friend of the family and whom Virginia knew as "Uncle Herbie," was the General Agent for Colonel Eskew's JE Ranch Rodeo company. He was barely five feet tall and walked with canes; but seemed to know everything about everything. Now Virginia admits he might have made up some of the things he told her. Uncle Herbie would go to a town ahead of the rodeo to start promoting and to set up photo shoots, interviews, and appearances for the performers. Often Eskew would give him instructions as to what he wanted to happen, and Herbie would make it happen. He was a colorful character whom everyone in rodeo at the time knew and admired. The blouse she wears was made by a fan who had a daughter similar in size to Virginia. Opal wrote to thank the woman and the two women corresponded for many years.

The Eskew family valued the Regers so much they were granted the privilege to travel in the caravan second in line, directly behind the owner of the rodeo. They also parked in this order, making it even more convenient for Virginia to learn from, and observe, the actions of the premier rodeo company in the east. The Reger children had the run of the rodeo, although often they were put to work picking up trash or other tasks. A lot of their time was spent watching performers practice, sewing costumes, and working with their horses. However, the kids often visited children's hospitals and orphanages to perform a few tricks for the kids and get their pictures in the paper.

Often, the afternoons left room for the cowboys and cowgirls to organize some horse racing. No doubt bragging rights were won and lost for the fastest horse and rider of the day. Also a jumping competition was regularly held, much like the more formal steeplechase racing, except with mobile hurdles. Virginia was fascinated with the jumping horses and their riders.

One woman seemed to fly over the obstacles on her horse. Hazel Hickey Moore travelled with the Eskew show and Virginia hung around watching so much, the woman and the little girl became friends. They talked for hours about positions, techniques and such. So often, in fact, Monte would avoid them as he got mighty tired of that talk. Hazel demonstrated her jumping techniques in detail for Virginia and often mounted the little girl bareback on her jumping horse to put her body in the proper positions for the various stages of the jump. Hazel confided in Virginia that she would love to compete in the English style steeplechase racing, but she had to be content with the Wild West Shows and rodeo. Here we see her near the "Wigwams" used in the shows. Below she is second from the right, among other cowgirls of the era.

That friendship lasted for years. Hazel and her husband took over a Wild West Show in Missouri when Monte took the family back to Oklahoma. In the mid 1950's, Virginia was performing in Saint Louis Missouri. Hazel saw the program and looked up her old protégé. By then Virginia was no longer jumping, but was a featured trick rider and roper. When the woman approached, she said, "Do you remember me?" Virginia recognized her voice and the two were happily reunited. But sadly, Hazel never got to see Virginia jump a horse.

Virginia would watch the races and practice for hours, noting the positions, techniques, and equipment used. Trick riding required leather loops be added to saddles to secure feet during a maneuver. But the jumpers had an English style riding saddle. As Virginia watched and learned an idea formed in her head. Bobby the longhorn steer was taught to jump over her father's old truck, and horses jumped over fences back in Oklahoma all the time. Why couldn't a horse be trained to jump over a car?

Everyone knew about the lady, Sonora Webster, who galloped her horse up a long ramp and jumped off a platform into water. She was a staple of the Atlantic City Steel Pier and other performers jumped horses into rivers with travelling circuses. Hazel Moore jumped her horse over just about anything and everything that got in her way. Virginia knew it was possible, she just had to prepare. Hazel was enthusiastic. Monte was excited to have another thrilling event to promote.

But what car would she jump? It seemed unlikely anyone would volunteer their vehicle for the act, so the answer was: use their own car. When the family pulled into the designated campground, the car was unhooked from the trailer so Monte could drive to publicity events, appearances, and radio shows. It wasn't needed while he was on duty as announcer. Virginia had her goal; she just needed to get to it.

When asked how does one train a horse to jump over a car, Virginia replied, "Well, you start out with something small and work your way up." It was decided. Over the winter in Oklahoma they would train horses to jump over small things and work their way up to cars.

In 1933, Monte performed with the JE Ranch Rodeo at the New York State Fair. Opal was in Heaven. She would get everyone going for the day in the morning, then disappear until late afternoon visiting all the amazing places and seeing the sights. This guide book contains almost 200 pages! This was a big fair. Below is one of her tickets from 1939.

The page stating Colonel Jim Eskew's rodeo would be an attraction during the first week has an interesting topic: Why do cowboys risk their lives riding bucking animals? Eskew's reply was, "The best cowboys...can make more money here in one week than they can by riding range for two years." That pretty well explains it.

This fair also featured steeplechase races which fascinated six year old Virginia. She didn't know at the time that she, too, would someday be sailing through the air on a horse.

Bobby was the first trained performing steer in the USA. By the time he retired, there were seventeen. By 1942, however, Bobcat Twister was getting a bit old and developed a large lump in his neck area. Monte had to put him down. He trailered his old friend to a vet in Oklahoma City, unloaded and walked to where the doctor was standing. The vet was nervous, but Monte told him it was ok, he would tell Bobby to lay down. Another man standing nearby scoffed sarcastically. But Monte gave the command and Bobby laid down. Amazed, the vet plunged the hypodermic needle into the tough hide, but Bobby didn't even flinch.

Monte couldn't bear to part with the prized animal and reason for his success. Bobby's head was sent to a taxidermist who mounted it like a trophy. That unusual wall hanging stayed with Monte until his death, then the head stayed on Virginia's dining room table for several months with her not knowing what to do with it. Then she decided to donate it to the National Cowboy and Western Heritage Museum in Oklahoma City

Below is a photo of the mounted head in Monte's trophy room about 1970. After Monte's death, Virginia explains it took several months to arrange for Don Reeves of the Museum to take it in as a donation. She specified it was to be protected at all costs. Meanwhile Bobby sat on Virginia's dining room table for weeks.

Finally, Don Reeves brought a station wagon. They almost couldn't fit those massive horns in the car! It took quite a bit of maneuvering, but they finally were able to take Bobby to his final resting place in the Museum.

Coming Into Her Own

The article below featuring Virginia was printed in "The Washington Post" on October 2, 1939. This was a result of an encounter Virginia had with a newsman who wrote this letter to ask her to write to him about her life on the road with the rodeo company. The following pages show the actual letter she wrote back to him, and the article as it was printed in the "Parade of Youth.

Parade of Youth
NEWS SERVICE

Jay Jerome Williams
Managing Director

August 23, 1938

1727 K St., N. W.
Washington, D. C.

Miss Virginia Reger
Buffalo, Oklahoma

Dear Virginia:-

Recently we heard of the part you take in Jim Eskew's Rodeo.

Will you please send us a detailed account of this, as well as your photograph, for Parade of Youth? It would be interesting to know how old you are, how long you have been with the Rodeo, how long you have had your pony, what his name is, what tricks you do with him, who taught them to you, whether you had any difficulty learning, whether you perform any stunts without your pony, if so, what they may be, whether you have ever gone to a regular school, how you like your correspondence school, what your friends think of your going to school by mail, whether you have any trouble keeping up with your lessons while touring with the show, what your life ambition is, what you are doing to attain it, what hobbies you have, etc. — in short, everything about yourself which you believe would be of interest.

The attached memorandum will give you further details regarding Parade of Youth.

Will you let me hear from you, please?

Sincerely yours,

Jay Jerome Williams

JJW/b
Encs.

Dear Mr. Williams,

    This is the first opportunity I have had to answer your letter asking for information about my life in the Rodeo. We have been busily moving about the country and in the past four weeks have been in Rochester, New York, Providence, Rhode Island, Albany and Elmira, New York. Now we are at the State Fair in Syracuse.

    I am ten years old and will be eleven October Thirteenth. Mother and Dad had me in a Saddle when I was only a few months old, in fact I was turned loose on a horse when only 8 month old. I fell off but didn't hurt myself.

Being around and on horses was as natural to me as most children's familiarity with a rubber ball and blocks. I started trick riding when I was eight, in 1936 when my family first came with Col. Eskew's show.

There are three of us you know, Dixie my sister who is seven and Buddy, my brother who is twelve. We do our act together so I thought you might like to know about them, too.

My pony's name is Pal, and he works right well in the arena. So far I've learned to do the Cossack stand, go around the horn, the one foot stand, the Russian drag, the crupper, double vault cart wheel and reverse crupper. Dixie does most of these and Buddy can do them all including a high crupper.

We all work our horses every morning and try to practice new stunts to add to the act. My ambition is to be one of the best trick riders in the country and I definitely do not want to ride buckin broncs. Dixie feels the way I do about it but Buddy wants to be a clown. He has already been in the arena doing a clown act with his mule but we left the mule back home in Woodward, Oklahoma this summer. He trained the mule himself and did pretty well.

He's going to rope calves and bull-dog, too. We all like to train animals and Daddy has one of the only Texas long-horns, with a routine that is very different and surprising. So you see, Daddy is able to teach us a lot about training all kinds of animals.

We like to spin ropes, but we don't do it the arena yet, just to amuse ourselves, and maybe someday we'll be good enough to do a rope act. My pony, by the way is a high-school pony, and maybe I'll train a high school horse when I'm a little older.

Mother helps us with our lessons which are from the Calvert

correspondence school in Baltimore. Lessons are pretty easy and we're ahead of most other kids our age.

Lots of people think our life a little irregular, but they've no idea how much fun we have. But don't think we don't work, and work hard. Its serious business having to show before thousands of people and if our pony refuses to work well, its embarassing, and we go ~~right back~~ in the back field and work him over again. If you let a pony get away with anything, even once, he'll continue to act up and I show him who's master right quick, before he's forgotten what he did wrong.

Sometimes we sell postal cards in the grand stand, and during the day we give other kids rides on our ponies for ten cents each. Half of the money goes in our bank account and the rest we keep for spending money. We pay for all our own ice cream cones and gum and things, which is fun, you know, to be independent like that.

My main hobby really is keeping a scrap book, newspaper clippings and accounts of radio interviews. We broadcast in most every town we visit. It's good training I suppose, but I don't like to talk about myself and get fussed sometimes.

We live right in the trailer on the fair grounds, and its very comfortable really. I'm just like most little girls and love pretty clothes. Mother makes all our dresses and all our riding clothes, too, and they are proud if I say so myself. Times though, I wish I could stay in old clothes and play, but the public likes to see us in our gay Western clothes.

Just one more thing, and most important. None of us would like to trade places with anyone we know. We love the life, and think of all the travelling we do. Everyone says that travel is an education in itself, and I agree, don't you?

Sincerely yours,
Virginia Ryan

The Washington Post

SECTION VIII | SECTION VIII

PARADE of YOUTH

WEEKLY SECTION — Copyright, 1938, Parade of Youth, Inc. — OCTOBER 2, 1938

Youngsters Thrill With Riding Skill

Born to the Saddle and How They Ride!

Two Girls and Boy Star in Circus Acts

Who says the circus is dying?

Three youngsters from Oklahoma don't think so. They're the Regers: Virginia, who will be 11 October 13; Buddy, 12, and Dixie, 7. The Regers are a one-family circus, and together with Mama and Papa Reger, scoot all over the country putting on their big little circus.

World Their Field.

They do trick riding on ponies. They go through intricate Cossack stands, Russian drags, cart-wheels, reverse croppers and double vaults. That's circus talk for tricks you've all seen.

The Regers have the true circus spirit. "The world," they boast, "is our territory! Satisfaction guaranteed, or no money!" Home is Buffalo, Okla., but you'll seldom find them there; they're always on the road.

Plenty of Fun.

"Lots of people think our life is a little irregular," writes Virginia, "but they've no idea how much fun we have.

"We live right in a trailer on the fair grounds, and it's very comfortable, really. I'm just like other girls and love pretty clothes. At times though, I wish I could stay in old clothes and play, but the public likes to see us in our gay Western costumes."

The Regers ride before they walk. "Mother and Dad had me in a saddle when I was only a few months old," continues Virginia. "In fact, I was turned loose on a horse when only 3 months old. I fell off but didn't hurt myself."

She Shows Him.

"We all work our horses every morning and try to practice new stunts. It's serious business if our ponies refuse to perform well. If you let a pony get away with anything, even once, he'll continue to act up. And I show him who's master right quick.

"Sometimes we sell post cards in the grandstand and during the day we give other kids rides on our ponies for 10 cents. We pay for all our own ice cream cones and gum and things; it's fun, you know, to be independent like that."

Newsfacts—There's just something about a circus: Frank J. Walter, of Houston, Tex., always wanted a circus. When he inherited a fortune, he spent $100,000 of it on a circus just to satisfy a boyhood whim. * * It has 142 animals, wagons, equipment, and kids all over Texas come to see it. They get in free!

Top, the Riding Regers: Buddy, Virginia and Dixie; Center, Buddy Cavorting in the Approved Cowboy Fashion; Below, Virginia at Ease!

Having grown up in rural Oklahoma, Virginia had no idea children could have grave illnesses and even die. Accidents happened at home, broken arms and such, but polio and cancer were shocking to the little girl. But Opal told her to not stare, keep a pleasant face forward, and to not act like anything was wrong. This photo was staged outside the hospital, then the group went in to perform. She did rope tricks on every floor with the Rogers Brothers, who were singers and bronc riders.

Over time, Virginia became accustomed to visiting hospitals where children with terrible diseases were treated, but she always kept a smile on her face and never asked any of the children what was wrong with them. She understood over time that bad things happen to kids sometimes, and has always been thankful for her health and well being even to today at age 89.

Training was ongoing out on the road. When Monte got a Shetland pony, Virginia was rather upset. She was used to Grandpa Crouch's big horses. Plus that pony wasn't very cooperative. He then came up with a similarly marked Welch/Shetland cross which Virginia loved. This was the horse named Pal mentioned in the letter. Monte and other rodeo cowboys and trick riders worked with the pony to teach him tricks.

One trick Pal learned was to lay down on the ground. Virginia would step gently onto the pony and raise her hand as if in victory. Then they'd get up and go do another trick.

This trick is called the "Tail Drag" or the announcers sometimes call it the "Death Drag" to be more dramatic. Feet are in loops secured to the back part of the saddle. At no time was Virginia tied to the horse. With feet flexed and ankles locked, she lowered herself backward, onto the horse's rump. After the prescribed time, she would then pull back upward, using legs and stomach muscles, but no hands. On this particular day, she wasn't feeling up to par, having a pain in her back from another day of trick riding. The grimace on her face shows the pain she was in, yet the show had to go on. Only if she were very ill was she excused from performing. On a few occasions, little Virginia would do her act, then promptly throw up and collapse back at the trailer.

Yet in all the years of trick riding, she only broke one bone. This occurred when a perfect storm of occurrences came about when she was fifteen. She was loping around the area, warming up her horse. Some men were dragging some bronc riding saddles across the area. This caused Virginia's horse to shy away from them. Unfortunately, there was a water leak near a fence and the horse slipped in the mud. Virginia bounced and hit her tailbone on the back, hard edge of the saddle and fell to the ground. When she stood, a terrible pain struck, and with each step it got worse.

The next day she couldn't even stand without assistance and rode home in the back seat of the car lying down. To the doctor they went and an x-ray was taken. The tailbone was cracked. There was no brace small enough for the tiny girl and the doctor suggested she wear a girdle.

Appalled, Virginia rebelled, but the pain scared her and made her fear not being able to ride again. Opal tried several places before finding one which carried a girdle small enough for the girl. She was horrified, but admitted the elastic contraption did ease the pain. With the heavy wool pants and summer heat, several girdles were needed to make it from laundry day to laundry day. She wore them all that year and some of the next, but never again put a girdle on her body.

Yet, when doing a trick where she had to land astraddle the saddle, she would land on that tailbone and cry out in pain. She learned to alter the remount to have both legs on one side of the saddle, then swing the other around to the proper position.

Years later, her second husband, Basil Morton, heard her speak of this. A memory flashed into his mind. It was his mother who sold the girdles to Opal Reger, and she bought a dozen of them at a time!

Virginia was never very ill, but contracted whooping cough one winter. She thought it would never end, and feared she might have asthma like her father. He often had coughing spells and asthma attacks.

When she was about four years old and staying with an aunt while her parents were gone for several weeks, Virginia learned the standard child's nightly prayer, "Now I Lay Me Down To Sleep." This she would say on her knees with hands in prayer position while her aunt was watching. One evening, the aunt was picking up some toys or straightening the stair landing where the children played and heard Virginia's little voice. She sneaked back to the doorway and found the little girl again on her knees with folded hands. Her prayer now was to tell God it was ok for her to be sick now and then when she was little, but to please not let her be sick when she was grown up, like her daddy. About fifty years later she heard this from her aunt, who was then very ill.

The prayer has worked so well that Virginia takes no prescription drugs and is quite healthy for an eighty-nine year old woman. Her back hurts often, but she manages the pain. And sometimes that cracked tailbone gets cranky in cold weather.

Virginia knew she had to cooperate with news people and photographers or she might not only get in trouble with her parents, but also lose her position trick riding in Eskew's rodeo. The photographer who took this photo was rather particular about how he wanted the picture to look. They were in the Chicago Coliseum parking lot so the situation wasn't ideal. Perhaps his camera lens wouldn't adjust, but he wished to get the feet of the ponies as well as the raised hands of the girl in the frame.

So he yelled to Virginia to bend her knees. Surprised, she balked as standing straight was proper form in the Roman Stand. But he said she was too tall. Irritated, she scrunched down and nearly lost her balance in the unfamiliar position. Plus, the phones were barely loping so he could keep up with them. Virginia said she realized then it was easier to ride the Roman Stand at a full gallop. It is unusual to see Virginia not smiling during an act, but , as she was quite uncomfortable, it is understandable.

But posing for the still photo, she was all smiles. This, too, was taken in the parking lot of the Chicago Coliseum aboard her favorite trick riding pony, Pal.

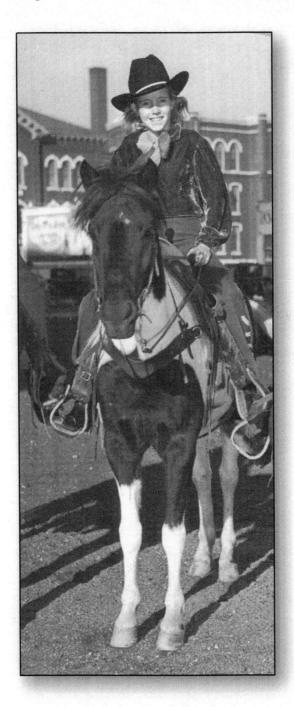

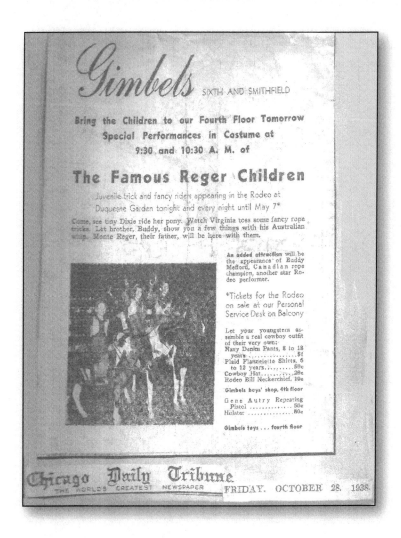

This advertisement in the Chicago Daily Tribune shows a typical result of Uncle Herbie's efforts at creating "buzz" about the performers before they even arrived in town. A publicity photo was obtained and event was planned for the Reger children without their knowledge. Virginia doesn't recall much about the store or the performance, but to a nine year old it was likely just another stop along the rodeo trail.

It is important to note they would not have worn costumes if shopping, sightseeing, or eating out. Opal endeavored to rise above the perceived "show people are low class" stigma by dressing in the local style and wearing a conservative hat and gloves. The family tried to blend in and only call attention to themselves during rodeo related affairs.

Back in Oklahoma, many events and fairs took the Regers to different events. On one occasion in Guyman, rain was falling down in sheets, but the parade carried on. Most of the participants huddled under various forms of rain gear, but not Virginia. She rode proudly and showed off her fancy parade costume.

Much like the four year old who would not take off her new coat for a photograph, the fourteen year old stood firm in her decision. It paid off—she got a check in the mail from the Pioneer Day event awarding her the best dressed in the parade!

On The Way Up

At home, Virginia put all the training together to successfully jump over a car on a horse. The next to last phase of that training was to jump over a hurdle. Note the horizontal bar on the wooden structure and over the car fender. After the horse cleared that hurdle with no problem, the next step was to pull the car into place. She practiced all day until the horse consistently flew over the car.

Then, of course, Monte called a photographer to come out to the ranch the very next day. It was then they noticed this horse made an unusual move. He would lift his back legs up in mid flight, causing his rump to raise up just a bit. Virginia could feel a little lift when he did that. That just added to the thrill of sailing through the air. It was as if he feared his back legs might hit the vehicle. But he never clipped a hood with his hooves.

She used an English riding saddle and always wore gloves while jumping.. A true jumping saddle like those used in steeplechase races had rolls of leather for the knees to grip. But Virginia made do with what she had.

This is the hurdle used to train the horse to jump. Over time the bar would be raised to the final level. During a performance, Virginia would first jump the horse over the hurdle, then the automobile would be driven into place. Most often Opal would drive, but occasionally they had to draft a passing cowboy to do the honors.

At a rodeo in Kansas, she was ready to do the act in public. Cars were lined up on one side of the designated arena area to create a boundary, which can be seen in the background of this photo. Two cowboys look on, one seems to be jumping with her. These were often other trick riders who would help out with the hurdle structure and other equipment. Monte was always in the announcer booth and was never on the ground when his children performed.

Over time, the girl became more and more confident and loved the sensation of flying through the air. Monte began marketing the act as a "Troup of Trick Riders, Ropers, High-jumping Horses, and Panhandle Pete, the Clown." When asked what "High School Horse" meant, Virginia replied, "I never really thought about it. It's just what they called a highly trained horse." It certainly isn't "elementary" for a horse to jump over a car!

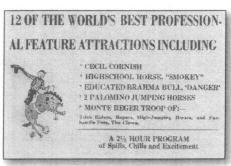

In this advertisement for the Little Rock rodeo, Virginia and her jumping palominos get a headline along with the famous "Stratosphere Man." This barrel chested former circus trapeze artist developed a unique act. A pole would be erected up to 150 tall and Arzeno Selden would do his trapeze acrobatics from a platform near the top of that pole. He would lash his feet to the pole and sway back and forth up to sixty feet, then a strap which was attached to a pulley on a wire was gripped in his teeth and he would "fly" with hands outstretched, following the wire all the way to the ground.

A flying man, Flying Chips, and Virginia Reger made for quite a lineup!

In 1940, Monte got the great idea to put on a Wild West Show Rodeo himself. He booked various venues and prepared to put on one right there at home. He set everything up on his own land which was just east of the city park and the small lake with "Crystal Beach." They had 100 head of stock, fifty cowboys and put on a real class show. At the end of that season, Lynn Beutler of Elk City, OK bought all of Reger's bucking stock and hired him to announce all the Beutler Brothers rodeos. That was a big step up for the self-made rodeo man. The family would tour with Beutler Brother Rodeos off and on for several years.

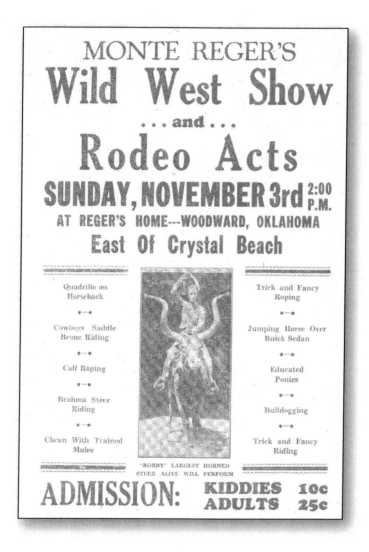

Always wanting Virginia to appear neat and stylish, Opal watched for opportunities to purchase durable fabric which also looked nice. She made the girls' blouses with full sleeves so the material would flutter like a flag as Virginia rode and moved in the arena. She often used bright colors of pink for her oldest girl.

All of Virginia's pants were made from wool, which may have stood up to rough wear, but proved to be quite warm in the summer. It was about this time Opal began putting appliques on the clothing, sometime the Reger name, sometimes symbols.

Virginia herself added something to the outfit. She fashioned ties to keep her hat on from shoestrings which were woven together. Then she frayed the ends to create a fuzzy type fringe. After using it and having other ladies admire the unique cord, Virginia made more in her spare time to give to friends at the rodeo.

Throughout the years, Virginia saved numerous flyers and programs where she and her family performed. As a young teenager, she must have been quite pleased to see her name listed among the best rodeo competitors and performers in the country.

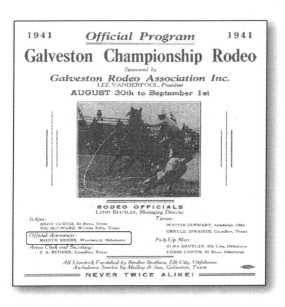

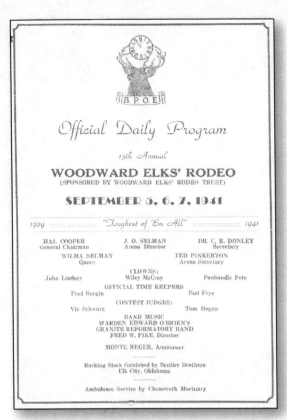

The very next week after the Galveston rodeo in September 1941, the Regers were back in Woodward for the huge Elk's Rodeo.

This is Monte's announcer copy of the program. He used an old, rickety typewriter to put in the names of the livestock drawn by the contestants. This was much easier to read than hand writing and fit better in the small spaces.

During Event seven, Virginia trick roped, in nine jumped over an automobile, then fifteen was her trick riding event. That made for a busy day for the fourteen-year-old.

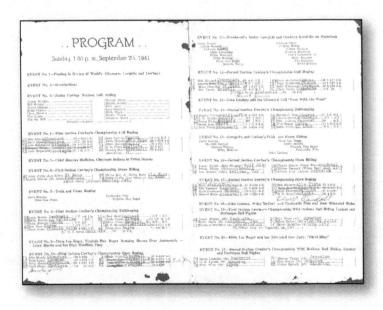

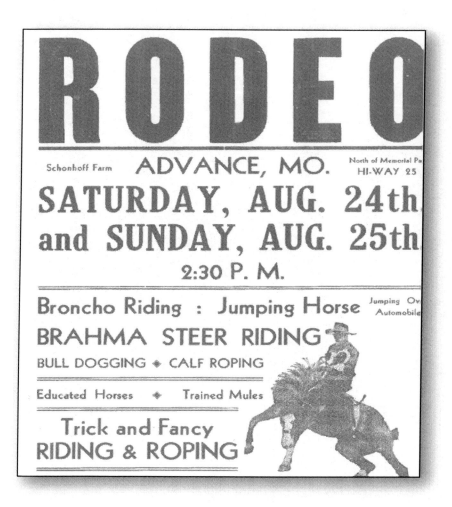

This is a sample of a flyer which might have been put in the window of a barbershop or in the area where the rodeo would be held. Notice the headlining "Jumping Horse Jumping Over Automobiles." All the Reger children could perform that stunt, but Virginia was the best at it, and loved it the most. Long after the other siblings no longer jumped, Virginia was still sailing over cars from coast to coast.

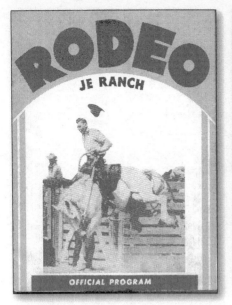

In Virginia's stacks of programs, many famous, and not so famous, names appear. But they all loved the sport, and the sport loved them. See the below information card from Madison Square Garden about the rodeo held in 1941. Prize money was at $36,820 which is almost $500,000 in today's money.

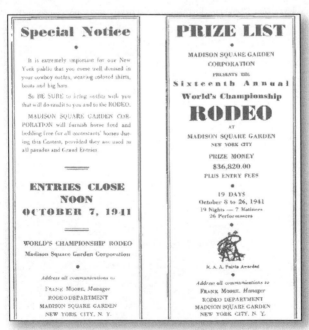

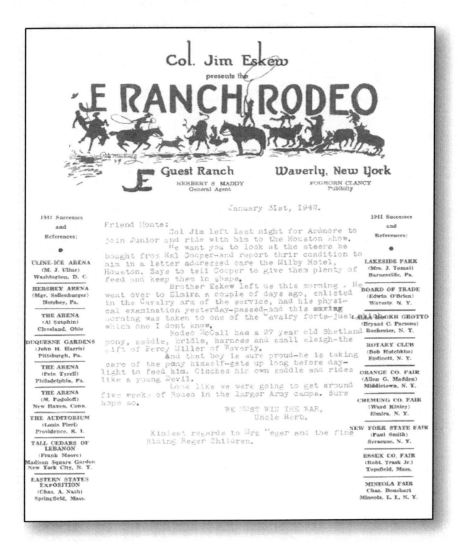

This letter from January 1942 includes instructions for Monte regarding some stock for the Houston, TX rodeo, and information Herbert was passing on from Colonel Jim. The statement "Brother Eskew...enlisted in the Cavalry…" speaks of Tom, one of Jim's sons who joined the service to support the war effort, much like thousands of other young men in America. He goes on to speak of a new act for the rodeo and the probable booking for five weeks of shows in large Army camps. He closes with "WE MUST WIN THE WAR," and regards to the Reger family. Note the letterhead which includes eighteen successful rodeo productions in 1941.

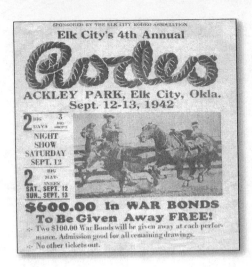

War was on every American's mind, even in this program from 1942. Using a War Bonds giveaway was a double win promotion. To buy one was $18.75 and it was redeemable after ten years at $25.00. The money went toward the war effort, which was vastly expensive. In today's currency the monetary cost of World War II is equal to over four trillion dollars!

Each member of the Reger family is featured in the program by name.

The back of the program claims people from forty-six states attended the Elk City rodeo in 1941, they could accommodate 6000 spectators, and have thirty acres of parking. Tickets were only .60 and you could get a box seat for an extra .50.

By 1943, Virginia was accustomed to having her picture in the paper, this one in Albuquerque, NM calling her a "top attraction" But this article is unique as the reverse side of the page contains a political cartoon depicting Hitler's revised view of a man he formerly admired, Italian dictator Musselini. The War was ever present.

Of course Monte had postcards made of his girls to sell. Hundreds of these were printed and Virginia had some in her possession as late as 2012. Selling postcards was part of the family business. All incoming monies went into the family fund, and probably saved a lot of the dollars from being spent on things the kids wanted at the time.

Monte bought a new car every year. With all the travelling the family did, miles stacked up fast. This 1946 Dodge served many purposes. Not only did Virginia and Flying Chips jump over it many times, it was often her dressing room, sleeping quarters, costume storage, and, of course, transportation. This vehicle has racks on the roof to secure the hurdle panels just as skiers would carry their long skis.

The car was prepared for the show with a fresh wash and wax. A reflection of a white fence can be seen on the side of the car above the clown.

Sometimes, another car had to be used if the Reger's wasn't available. Here is Virginia flying over the hood of a 1941 Ford convertible owned by one of the rodeo directors. She now states it was a bad habit of looking into the car and wondering, "Who are all those people?" when she should have been watching where she was going!

During Virginia's senior year in high school, a dance instructor wanted to put an act in a USO show at the nearby Woodward Army Air Corps base. The man stated he worked with the famous dancer, Gene Kelly, and Virginia thought he resembled Kelly. He recruited girls who had background in dance and trained his troupe to do a routine.

Being on the base was fun for the girls with all those men in uniform and the airplanes flying in and out. Pilots were trained in B-29 Super fortresses and other bombers in the small facility which became a municipal airport after the war. Virginia also trick roped on stage and was one of the acts in the revue with included other dancers and singers.

One of Virginia's high school friends met a soldier from that base and married him. He was from New Jersey and that's where they went after the war. About fifteen years later, Virginia was taking part in a fashion show at Marshall Fields in New York City modeling western wear. Helping the models with their clothes was that friend from Oklahoma! She and Virginia had a little reunion right there in the back stage area. The friend had lost all her Oklahoma accent and was very happy living and working in New York City. The models seems shocked that the two knew each other, and even more surprised the friend was from Oklahoma. Virginia then noticed something. Prior to that moment, none of the models paid any attention to her friend, like she was just a fixture. But after they saw she and Virginia together, they were more open and friendly. Seeing the natural friendliness of two gals from Oklahoma created an openness where the friend was then accepted by the models.

Following in the footsteps of Jean Harlow, Carole Lombard, and other Hollywood blondes, Virginia bleached her hair and instantly became a glamor girl herself. Despite looking the part, she was still the all American cowgirl, drinking, not wine or Coca Cola, but a quart of milk three times per day!

Here the blonde trick rider looks down at a cowboy who appears to be just about ready to jump out in front of her. Imagine the look on her face, freezing him in place. It was imperative to not distract the horse from executing a perfect landing or disaster could ensue. Notice the large tents in the background which were often used to provide a boundary for the area designated in an open field for the arena. It also protected area for grandstands keeping the spectators in the shade.

The Reger family often performed for benefits on military bases. This photo was taken at the Lubbock Army Flying School which was ten miles west of the City of Lubbock and later became Reese Air Force Base. This was a newly constructed facility on the flat land of the West Texas plains specifically designed to train flying cadets. Over 7000 pilots graduated from this program and went on to fly bombers and fighters in both Europe and the Pacific theaters of war.

Virginia remembers they could bring their horses onto the base if they agreed to "clean up" after them. So most often they stuck with rope tricks to entertain the servicemen. When they would visit hospitals, often the doctors would tell about a patient's injury or illness. Sometimes the man would not be expected to live much longer, plus, was not aware of his situation. The sixteen-year-old felt very strange looking at and talking with a man who might not be alive the next day. She wished the doctors wouldn't have revealed that information, as it made her mighty uncomfortable. But, professional that she was, Virginia put on a brave face and performed her tricks for the sick and injured and brought them a moment of joy in their dire circumstance.

As previously mentioned, Virginia did not drink soda pop, but she and Monte were asked to pose for photos to use in the Oklahoma Roundup for a Coca-Cola ad. Here she holds the drink and Joy Sandra stands by.

Below is a letter, thanking Virginia and Monte for doing the photo shoot.

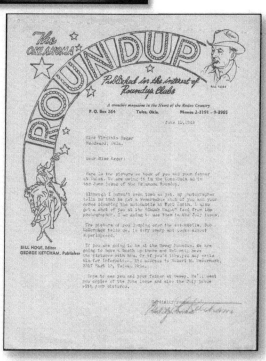

In 1944, Virginia became sick with a case of flu which leaned toward pneumonia. She was ordered to bed by their Woodward doctor. But she had a contract to perform at the Houston rodeo for Vern Elliott. He was well known in the business and she was anxious to make a good impression and get more contracts in his shows.

Further, the Houston arena was arranged in a circle, where the riders performed their tricks down one long straight stretch, then turned the horse sharply to come back up the other side. Most arenas of the time were just straight tracks with no turning.

The headstrong young woman convinced Opal to take her to Houston to perform. She worked upwards of twenty performances, but after each one, Opal practically carried her daughter to the hotel, put her to bed, and tried to keep her going.

A hotel clerk suggested she drink malted milk with a raw egg mixed in. That drink gave her energy and he fixed three of them per day for her. All other food wouldn't settle, but that did. Virginia's trick riding career was the most important thing in the world and nothing was going to stop her.

Breaking Into The Big Time

As the war in both Europe and the Pacific heat up to fever pitches, patriotism ran deep in the United States. People longed for something good, and the rodeo coming to Dallas, Texas offered that opportunity. In conjunction with Armistice Day, which dates from World War I, thousands of people tried to get into the rodeo. Over 6000 men and women witnessed the contestants and performers, with 2000 being turned away from the Fair Park Grandstand. And there was seventeen year old Virginia, riding and roping before the biggest crowd she'd ever faced.

Memphis Press-Scimitar

Prize Animals Are Having Their Hour At Fair's Rodeo and in Show Ring

Monte obtained some fine Palomino horses which were used for showing and performing. This is one of the show horses, Joy Sandra, which was also used in trick riding, where the horse she used for jumping was called "Flying Chips." This Memphis reporter believed both of them were "good-looking" despite her being in "practice clothes" and with her hair in a scarf. She confesses there were likely curlers under that scarf and she NEVER went out with curlers in her hair.

Throughout the war years, the family performed in many USO type shows for veteran's hospitals in Oklahoma and New Mexico. The patients were brought to the arena in wheelchairs and even ambulances. For those unable to attend, photos of the Reger horses were shown to the patients, while Virginia and her sister dressed in costume and twirled ropes for the bedridden veterans.

Opal kept busy not only sewing costumes for the three children, keeping them clean was almost a full time job. All the pants were wool dyed into bright colors such as pink, red, and blue, fabrics she picked up in New York by the bolt. Some was lighter weight like those in a men's suit. But most was heavier weight, especially during WWII . And it all required dry cleaning. That being mush too expensive, Opal simply stopped at a gas station and purchased a cleaning fluid such as Stoddard's and did the cleaning herself. The girls had enough costumes to wear something different each time they entered an arena for consecutive ten days. That's a lot of laundry.

In 1945, the Woodward Elks couldn't afford to hold a pageant for rodeo queen. At the last minute, they asked Monte if Virginia would serve as queen. Being an officer of the rodeo, he agreed. But Virginia was not happy about it. In her experience, the rodeo queen was just a beauty queen, not a true rodeo performer. She practically threw a fit, but was informed she HAD to do it, for the rodeo. Duty won her over and she finally agreed. The announcement hit the paper and was picked up by a news service which released the story to over 700 newspapers.

The opening night she was presented with a rather sad bouquet of flowers. Apparently the committee's money completely ran out and they begged a nosegay of scrap flowers from the local florist. She led the parade with it in hand, and participated just as she was expected. After that first night, she threw the bouquet in the trash. One of the committee members retrieved it. He hurried to her with instructions to use the same, sad bunch of flowers every night. Disgusted, she made the best of it and cooperated. But after the third and last night of the rodeo, the flowers were beyond wilted and bedraggled and it took everything she had not to throw them into the dirt and let the horse step on them. But always cognizant of people watching, she waited until she was in private and gave the bouquet a hearty sendoff into the trash.

The beautiful girl and her gorgeous, athletic horse., Flying Chips. Having mostly Thoroughbred blood, the horse was a natural jumper. Quoted in a news article in 1945, Virginia stated, "He likes to jump, and often jumps high hurdles in his pasture just for his own amusement. It's not hard to train them if you're gentle and patient." The English riding saddle was a war trophy brought back her brother.

Flying Chips sailed over cars for several years before he had a problem. Virginia had several other jumping horses, but he and another palomino, Yellowstone, were her favorites.

In 1948 in Little Rock, a heavy rainstorm delivered a downpour on the arena grounds. As long as the car could be driven into the arena without getting stuck, it was assumed the horses could keep their footing. But Chips did lose his footing as he approached the car. His legs hit the hood of the car and flipped end-over-end over the car. Virginia jumped to the side and remounted.

He was obviously hurt, so she didn't make him try the jump again. Meanwhile, the car was stuck in the mud, and some other horses were used to pull it out of the arena. The hood was torn loose and had to be tied down to take it to a garage to be repaired.

Oklahoma Pinup Gal

Here's your pinup from the plains of Northwestern Oklahoma. Miss Virginia Mae Reger, Woodward beauty. Just turned 17, this brown-eyed blonde will rule as queen of the world famous Woodward Elks rodeo which is scheduled there on August 17-18-19. (NEA TELEPHOTO).

    This is the photo and article the news service sent to all those newspapers, unbeknownst to the seventeen year old Virginia. Some of those papers made their way to servicemen around the world still on duty after the war was over. They picked out her name and the fact she was at the Woodward Elks rodeo and addressed letters to her. She got letters from young men wanting one of her "Pin Up" pictures! One even vowed to come see her when he got back to Oklahoma from Czechoslovakia.

    Virginia and Opal tried to answer every one of the over 100 letters received as a result of this story and several wrote back to her. However, the one who vowed to come to Woodward to have her "learn him how to ride a horse," did not follow through. He likely considered her daddy might object.

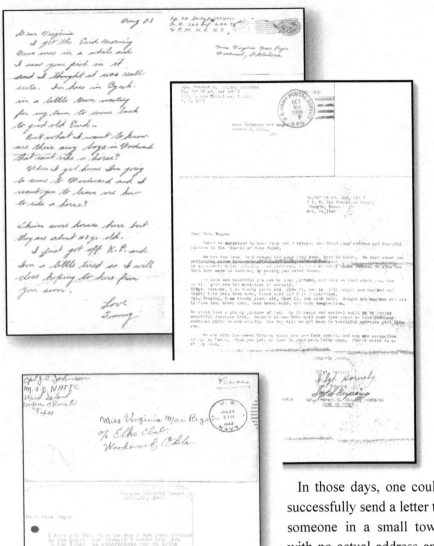

In those days, one could successfully send a letter to someone in a small town with no actual address and the envelope would be delivered. These men got Virginia's name and location from the article, and she got their letters.

Virginia started keeping her own records and even going out on her own (with Opal as chaperone) at age seventeen. These are pages from a notebook from 1946 showing the places she performed, number of performance, and amount paid.

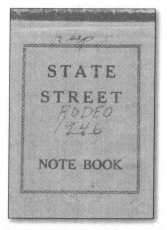

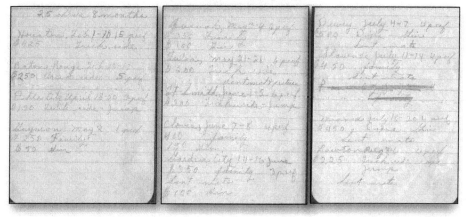

In Houston, February 1-10 for fifteen performances they were paid $425 for trick riding. That equals over $5,500 in today's money!

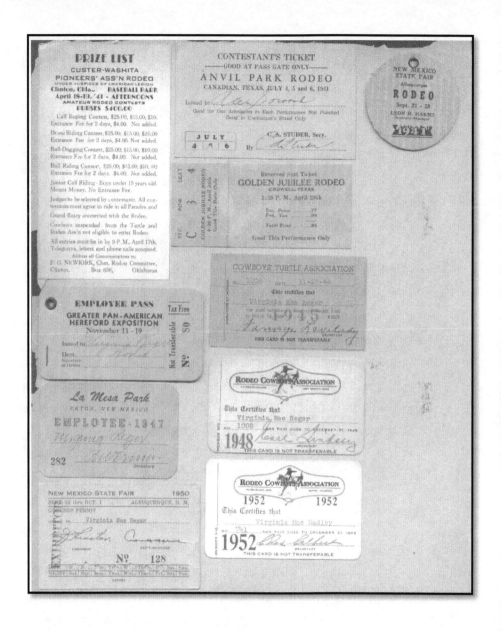

The next three pages show the participant cards Virginia received through the years. This shows many of the places she performed.

Virginia almost always was selected to carry the American flag in parades and grand entry ceremonies. Different sizes were used at different times—the top photo shows a huge flag which seems to have a pole twelve feet long. Her sister carried the flag of the state in which they were performing. Often great fanfare was involved, such as is shown below in the Buffalo Bill Rodeo Days photo. A local man assumed the visage of the famous cowboy and rode in the parade near Virginia.

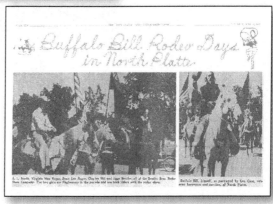

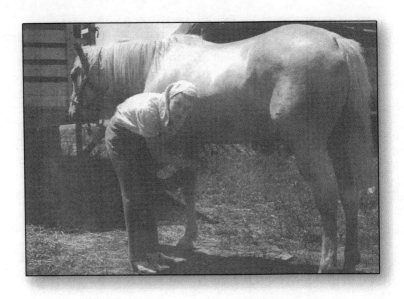

Caring for the horses was always a priority. Here Virginia is caught unaware by a passerby who later gave her this photograph. The well trained horses knew how to cooperate and rarely gave any trouble. With many of the events being held in an open field, the possibility of picking up a rock or thorn in the horse's hooves was high. A quick cleaning ensured there would be no problems during the performance. After all, when the horse made a landing after jumping over a car, or you were doing a manuever while it ran, you needed to be certain all four feet were in tip-top shape.

Knowing to never appear in public with curlers in her hair, Virginia commonly used a scarf to cover her head, gather the long hair, and tie it tightly to secure all under the fabric so her hair would look good later, even when she was upside down.

Virginia Mae Reger, Woodward, Okla., rides her jumping horse, Chips, over an automobile, making a spectacular jump of 4 feet 9 inches, and 22 feet broad to clear the car. You will see Miss Reger, and other star performers, during the Third Annual Crosbyton Rodeo

When her reputation grew, Virginia often was billed as a top performer and a photo like this would appear in the local paper. This reporter went a step further and spelled out the statistics of the jump. The horse would be almost five feet off the ground and sail twenty-two feet from the start of the jump to the landing.

Picture a parking lot with painted spaces. With a width of the average eight feet, the horse would take off at one stripe, clear two more stripes before landing at the far edge of the third space. That's covering some ground!

At the fairs and rodeos, there were always many activities and events. Often horse shows would occur and Virginia was right in there with her palomino. She won many trophies and enjoyed every minute. Here she is looking all grown up and ready to be a solo performer.

She was only seventeen when she booked her own gigs, was just beginning to drive and didn't have her own car, so Opal took her to the events and served as chaperone. A young, single girl simply did not travel alone It was then she started making a name for herself, separate from the Reger Family. Her initials were stitched on almost every costume—the "V" and "R" show prominently on the white jacket lapels.

Notice the white saddle and rigging on Joy Sandra. Virginia dyed her saddle white to have it be more showy in the arena. Once when touching it up behind the fence before a performance, the white shoe polish tipped over and as she grabbed at it, the liquid splashed onto her face, hair and clothing.

A nearby cowboy who never laughed burst out in laughter at the sight. Almost in a panic, she ran to her hotel room. A maid there saw her and hurried to her own home to get supplies to help clean up the mess. Virginia was so thankful for her help, she arranged for passes to the rodeo to be delivered to the hotel maid. It was shortly after this Virginia opted for a red hair color. By then the white saddle trend had caught on, so she also planned to redo her favorite saddle to black and silver to stay unique..

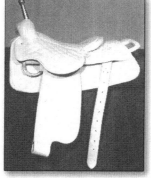

The enterprising young woman who sold postcards when she was four years old naturally saw an opportunity with Christmas Cards. After graduating from high school, Virginia thought she should go to business school during the winter months off the rodeo circuit. To fund her way through, she sold these cards to various stores along the road to Enid. She found it easy to sell, noticing when the store owner was distracted or occupied and she would close in for the sale. They almost always bought cards, even if the ones she sold them the previous week had not sold.

At the business school, she sat through classes and had an epiphany when the instructor told the women how much money they could make per year as secretaries. She realized she could make the same amount of money in just a few rodeos and quit the school right then.

Vital to a performer's portfolio were photos to send to rodeo producers. Over the years, Virginia had many such photographs taken in many different costumes, but no others while perched on a chair which was hidden under a blanket. Obviously in the photo on the right she got tickled at the situation!

The post-war years brought great economic growth to all types of industry in the USA. Dallas was emerging as a leader in trade and this magazine was companion to the markets springing up there. A photographer grabbed Virginia and another girl, plus two men who were hanging about, dressed them in green coveralls and staged this photo. The man leaning on the fence was a lingerie salesman who frequented the back stages of the rodeo. The mule belonged to a clown and was simply tied to the fence. Notice the animal raising its foot, as if it expected to have the hoof get a cleaning or trim.

As this was one of the many times Virginia was posed in a photograph, she never dreamed it would show up on the cover of a magazine. Especially the one which was given to all vendors selling apparel at the market. She also at first hated wearing the coveralls, but got to keep them and found the one-piece all purpose attire to be quite convenient and functional. She would throw it on to run to the barn to care for the horses, and then return to get properly dressed. That first set actually wore out and she so enjoyed the practicality, another was soon purchased.

Audie Murphy, the most decorated soldier of World War II was also well known in rodeo arenas. He was to receive an award at the Fort Worth Fat Stock Show and Rodeo, a huge event which has today run over 120 years. Virginia was asked by the head of that rodeo, Mr. Watts, to present the award to the hero. And when Mr. Watts asked you to do something, you did it.

The trouble came when Virginia found out where the award was to be given and how she was to get there. A platform was placed above the pens where the bulldogging steers were kept. A 2 x 6 plank was stretched across another pen. When Virginia saw that she nearly fainted. The steers were moving around, horns banging on the sides of the pens. And they wanted her to walk across a six inch wide plank above them. She couldn't do it.

She told Mr. Watts she just couldn't walk across that plank. Why? She was afraid of heights! Incredulous, he called a few other men to listen. The famous, fearless trick rider who jumped horses over cars was afraid of heights? The men laughed and laughed.

But Virginia had an answer for them. She suggested Cecil Cornish, a very talented trick rider whose balance was uncanny. He could ride Roman style, jumping back and forth and not fall off the running horse. She did meet Murphy—on the ground— but did not walk the plank to present that honor to him.

Letters were always coming in for portfolio photographs for publicity, consideration for contract, and sometime just from curiosity about the young woman's life.

One such request came from a source which wanted photos of Virginia "in her dressing room getting ready." Dressing room? Did they not know she most often dressed in the car or restroom at the rodeo? She supposed the requestor pictured a movie star type trailer with fancy furniture and a dressing table.

But wishing to comply, Opal and Virginia staged a "dressing area" in the Reger's living room. They hung several of her costumes from the chair rail on the wall, arranged some suitcases to serve as a table, and rested a hat here and there in the vignette. The young woman then "acted" like she was preparing for an appearance while the photographs were being taken. Both women thought the situation terribly funny, and laughed about these photos for many years. The dressing room in the living room was a memorable moment!

Virginia almost always made personal appearances, many times one right after the other, in the town where the rodeo would be playing. Stores, local attractions, and even radio spots. This 1948 photo was taken in Winston Salem where a remote radio broadcast was held. For days before the event had been publicized on the station and many people turned out to see the beautiful rodeo star. Someone asked to try on her hat, then the photographer wanted to take the picture, else she would have been sporting a large black western hat to compliment her outfit. This is also an example of how she would dress outside the arena, tasteful and classic, with just a hint of western flair.

Here in a blouse made from lace covered with a silver sequined, zipped vest, she poses holding the hat. Virginia much preferred wearing the hat, but followed the photographer's instructions knowing they would remember her as cooperative and easy-going. She also had a gold sequined vest worn in the same manner.

In February, 1950 a wild leopard escaped from the Oklahoma City Zoo. This article from the Chicago Tribune show the massive news exposure the event received. For three days people all over Oklahoma thought they saw the animal and many calls were made to radio stations about the sightings.

After three days the leopard returned to the zoo, hungry and tired, but, sadly, was euthanized. But the incident inspired Virginia when she saw some animal print velvet. A western style yolk was designed and the velvet was applied to accent the forest green wool suit. She was trying the outfit on to measure for the pant hems to the right length for her boots. The family was just about to leave for Denver to attend a convention where the business of rodeo was conducted and contract acts were booked. Some friends stopped by on their way to Colorado and insisted on taking this photo behind the Reger home. She successfully negotiated and renewed several contracts at this annual convention and no doubt wowed the promoters with her hand made western suit with velvet leopard print yolk

While appearing at the 1949 Fort Worth Fat Stock Show and Rodeo, Virginia was interviewed about her costumes. Three women riders were featured, Tad Lucas, , Bernice Dossy, and Virginia. The photo was staged on some stairs, and Bernice pretended to trip just as the picture was taken so she could step in front of Virginia. By the look on her face, you can see she wasn't pleased about being upstaged!

THEY MAKE THEIR OWN—These three trick and fancy riders, make their own colorful riding habits. Tad Lucas, right, wears a turquoise suit fringed in bright red leather and silver nail heads. Virginia Reger's, left, outfit is fashioned in pink wool with a light blue over-check detailed in white fringe over-stitched in blue leather. Bernice Dossey, right, shows off her white wool gabardine suit with trousers and blouse fringed in bright green. They wear a pin or scarf at the neckline.

Tad Lucas, the famous cowgirl of the time, usually dressed in red. Her husband would go up into the spectator stands and watch her during practice to determine which costume she should wear in the performance. The color of the dirt, the lighting, and other attributes factored into his decision which was aimed at making her the most noticed rider in the rodeo.

Often many circus and carnival acts were looking for work. With a quick costume adjustment to a Western Style, they landed jobs as feature acts at rodeos around the country. Above is the husband and wife team, Jack and Bobby Knapp. They were small people who were highly talented and trained in acrobatics. When he threw her into the air as shown above, she would do a flip before landing in "the splits." Limber is not a big enough word for what she is doing in the top right photo.

Below is another circus act which found a home in rodeo. Again a little Western flair to their outfits and the trained dogs were a hit with all the rodeo audiences and participants. Virginia remembers them all as very nice people.

The Beeswax Moore Family, as pictured above, bring to you one of the fastest and most entertaining dog acts in the business today. This act is appealing to all, as this happy-go-lucky gang runs rampant in a comical, riotous act. While stressing comedy the Moore Family feature many outstanding feats as their 4-legged friends go through their paces in an enlightening manner.

Virginia favored light colored blouses with wide, flowing sleeves in the belief they showed well and the billowing of he sleeves made her appear to be moving faster. This is a light blue blouse paired with blue pants sporting white fringe. Opal had the idea to use felt for fringe which was much more sturdy than braided thread fringe.

About this time Joy Sandra was expecting a foal. Virginia worked her well into the pregnancy until one day when she was cinching the saddle into place, the horse reacted unexpectedly. Apparently the cinch was pinching her badly that Joy Sandra turned and bit Virginia on the back. The bite tore her blouse and broke the skin. The young woman loosened the cinch and went on with the show. After that rodeo, the horse was stabled at the Reger ranch where she delivered that foal. But Virginia needed Joy, and they found a big plow mare with milk to spare and put the colt on that animal. Virginia wanted to keep that colt, but being out on the circuit she couldn't. The big mare and little palomino colt were an odd couple, but sold for a good price.

Appearances at children's homes and hospitals had always been part of travelling with the rodeo for Virginia, and it was no different as she became a woman performer. Of course, there was always the opportunity for publicity, but seeing the little children in those dire circumstances always touched her heart. Here she stands with Joy Sandra while a troup of orphans line up to take turns riding around the courtyard. Notice the boy's uniform — a set of overalls made from a striped material which resembles bed ticking. Each face tells a sad story and Virginia was there to brighten part of their lives.

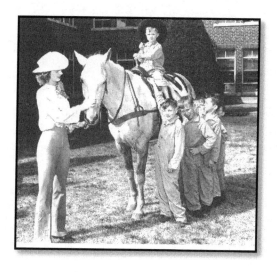

Below Virginia and her sister line up ready to ride in the rodeo parade. The white suits and white saddle rigging contrast nicely with the dark horses.

Living The Dream

Driving from rodeo to rodeo was part of the life. Virginia was earning around $20,000 per year as a performer, so the satisfaction of being a top billed act was well worth the effort. And earning such a great amount of money added to her independence. That's over $150,000 in today's money!

However, she endured such questions as, "How early do you have to get up in the morning?" and "Isn't it true that air is so fresh out in the open spaces that it's hard on people to breathe all that clean air if they're not used to it?" And after one particularly long ride of 600 miles in 1950 to get to a rodeo where she had been booked, she approached the announcer, a well known and respected person in rodeos of the day, and tried to describe her act so he could intelligently announce it.

Unfortunately, he was busy and distracted and failed to pay her any attention. Furious and tired, and lonely having driven so far with only her horse to talk to, Virginia stomped off. Later that evening she stepped into the arena and performed her acts. That announcer, Tom Hadley, was love-struck. He remembered seeing her at rodeos. Over a month later they were at the same rodeo and he asked her out to the movies and only a few months later proposed.

They married on December 26, 1950, and when rodeo season began in 1951, they went about their jobs together or separately, as the contracts they secured required. On May 12, 1953, Mathew James Hadley was born. Virginia gained only a few pounds with the pregnancy, per her doctor's instructions. She delivered a healthy baby boy, and after only six weeks, fit back into her costumes and returned to the rodeo circuit. Some time after that, she stated she wouldn't do that again! But when her second son, Mark, was born in 1958, she did do it again. It was only six weeks off and back to the rodeo she went with two boys in tow. One thing she had to alter was how she packed. With all the kids' things, she condensed her costumes to be interchangeable separates and thus saved a lot of room in the suitcases. She started each of the boys roping at age two. A second generation rodeo family was now on the road.

In 1951, the first year she and Tom were married, twenty-three year old Flying Chips was in the show to jump the car—a car Tom had recently purchased. The arena was in a grassy field, and the horse kept slipping during the take off and almost fell several times on the landing. Tom was announcing this All Girl Rodeo and made a decision..

After Virginia did her trick riding act, she saw a young woman leading Flying Chips. She hurried over to thank the woman for catching him, assuming he escaped from the pen. When she reached for the lead rope, the woman pulled it away. "This is my horse! I just bought him." "Bought him? He wasn't for sale!" Virginia replied. The woman pointed to the announcer stand. "He sold him to me." Shocked, Virginia watched as her performing horse of over fifteen years was led away. He wasn't registered, so she had no recourse. When asked how she felt about it, her reply was, "I almost left Tom Hadley right then and there!" Helpless, she shed tears at the loss of her old friend, Flying Chips.

Virginia landed a long-term contract with the Steiner rodeo company, and was often invited to dinners and events. While in Baton Rouge, LA, she joined the Steinters dining with the Sheriff of East Baton Rouge Parish. This card was presented to her as an honorary member of the sheriff's office.

A meal was served. The Sheriff was proud to state that the staff of the jail ate the same food as the inmates and he was serving that food to his guests. After one bite, Virginia's stomach almost turned over. She looked at the other people, all had the same reaction except the Sheriff. He was still going on about how it was the same food as the prisoners ate.

Though she tried to be polite, the meal was so entirely bland, it was like eating cardboard. Perhaps in Louisiana they expected a little more flavorful meal, but that was not to be at the Sheriff of East Baton Rouge's table.

Lake Charles American Press

Beverly Steiner, wife of Tommy the rodeo producer, liked to get publicity and took every opportunity to get herself and her boys into the newspapers. After getting the two youngsters dressed up in their fancy outfits, the woman began readying herself for the photo shoot which was to take place in the lobby of the hotel.

The boys were being boys, roughhousing and acting silly. Irritated, Beverly told the younger one to sit down somewhere, anywhere, and be still until she was ready. Being in the bathroom, the boy sat on the toilet and promptly slid into the water. But they were late and there was no time to change. So his picture was taken with wet pants!

1955 also was the year Wrangler featured Virginia in their "Blue Bell Wranglers." She always used bright colors in her costumes, and more subtle hues in "street clothes." Jeans in seven different shades was right up her alley.

For this pose, the photographer's helper pinned the pant legs close to Virginia's skin and handed her a misshapen, black hat. She was instructed to put it on the back of her head, in a very unnatural position. Appalled at the appearance of the hat and the ridiculous directions, Virginia took action. She immediately began shaping the hat, quite the task with no tools or steam, but she got it into a semblance of a western brimmed hat. Then she told them she would NOT wear it as they instructed. The Wrangler representative said, "You work for us, do what we say." Virginia replied, "You want a rodeo cowgirl, don't you? This is how we wear a hat." With that hat in place she stood her ground. The men backed down.

But one other request was for her to prop a foot up on the fence rail. She didn't have a problem with that, but thought 'if one of those pins pokes me...' The photo shoot was a success and the ad used in many different magazines. Wrangler sent her color jeans and other clothes for several years thereafter.

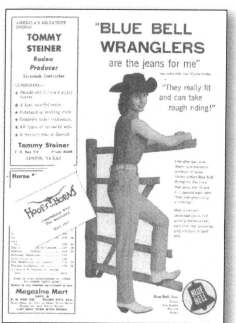 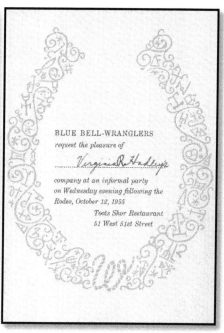

Virginia's schedule was always filled with appearances and invitations such as this one to a party at a New York City restaurant notorious for catering to males and not welcoming "wives."

After it seemed everyone was using a white saddle, Virginia decided it was time to change hers. Loving the frame, she arranged for a layer of padding with quilted, black leather covering to be added. Silver stitching would stand out against the black. The result was a striking look which got a lot of attention in many different situations.

The unusual rope loop photo was carefully staged for Wrangler. The photographers often took many photos of which only a few were chosen for use.

Below is an ad with models in the sweaters she designed for Panhandle Slim Western Wear.

Virginia favored high necks and shiny things. Often she wore a scarf and or a brooch at her throat. This ensured no embarrassing accidents would happen while hanging upside down or riding at full speed. The above photos were taken by fans and show another of her versatile costumes. The lace top zipped to the lighter colored midriff section, was assembled into one piece and zipped up from behind.

Often doing a quick change in a corner or even the car, Virginia occasionally needed help with the back zipper. Sometimes she would ask Mat to zip up her costume. He didn't like doing that, and would often hail a passing cowboy, "Hey, come zip up my Mama!' Of course, the cowboy would oblige.

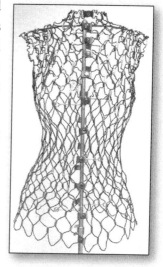

During the off season, lots of designing and sewing took place. Virginia had this type of dress form, which could be pressed into shape around the body and then unfastened to use as a true form for fitted clothing. This is how she got the blouses to fit so perfectly.

But sometimes she had a hard time locating the form as her mother and aunt also loved to use it. In a family of seamstresses, Virginia had to wait for her turn with the adjustable, wire dress form. It was on this she created her mix and match costume pieces for a more versatile and easily carried wardrobe.

Another rodeo gal who is becoming known as a designer—but who up to now has designed only her own clothes—is Virginia Hadley, also a genuine rodeo personality. She is a trick rider, and she and her husband, who is a rodeo announcer, follow rodeo most of the year. Virginia and Tom design their own clothes—Tom was the first one I heard mention the Western tuxedo—he had a black and a white one. Virginia was one of the first ones to come out with the lace shirt—with a sequined camisole underneath—like the fancy outfit Nancy Sheppard showed in the June-July issue.

Last winter Virginia designed the Western sweater that I have already mentioned and sold the idea to Panhandle Slim. It is now in production and will soon be on the market and I predict a big hit. The sweaters are washable orlon in luscious pastels and of course red and white. The yokes, pockets and collars are of washable cotton twill or Indian head in either a matching shade or slightly darker color—a rich toast on a beige sweater, for instance. Comes in men's too, in beautiful grey tones—handsome, warm and conservative—also has trousers to match. Imagine how comfortable, warm and packable these sweaters will be.

Western sweater manufactured by Panhandle Slim, created by Virginia Hadley. Pants are the colored Wranglers. Tom has on one of the man's sweaters worn without a shirt. The leather carved tie is something new which Virginia is putting on the market. Some have rhinestones set in leather.

Left is Virginia and Tom in the sweaters she designed for Panhandle Slim. Lower left is a more unusual set of sleeves from a harlequin print satin.

Always designing and using up every scrap of fabric, Virginia fashioned some interesting costumes. Above is an outfit with cream colored insets in the sleeves and legs, fringed tassels, and conchos.

When Roy Rogers' wife, Dale Evans, saw this suit, she fell in love with it and wanted one just like it. Trouble was, it had been made from various scraps from other projects and likely couldn't be duplicated.

The black light act began with flood type lights in 1951. Virginia experimented with those for a while before finding long, fluorescent tube black lights in Dallas. One could find an abundance of theatrical type equipment and fabrics there. She painted her boots and belt with a brush and paint that would glow under the lights. Once perfected, she used the act all over the country, though transporting the four foot long lights was tricky. .

Virginia received an offer from MCA to perform the act in some of their productions, which she turned down. Travelling with the kids to rodeo was one thing. Leaving them to do something like this was another. The mother in her demanded she say with her family.

This is the belt she painted in 1951. Her waist size was a tiny twenty-one inches!

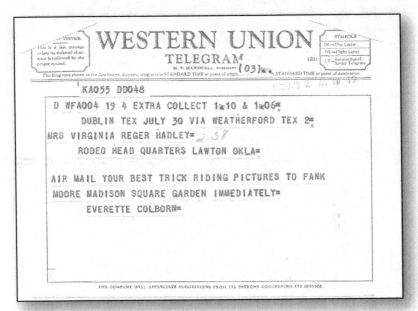

In August of 1955, Virginia received an important telegram. Everett Colborn wanted her to appear in his Madison Square Garden rodeo! Sending the photos by air mail ensured the quickest possible delivery. It was the 30th Anniversary of that most famous of rodeos and Virginia was returning twenty-one years after she first saw the Garden with her father.

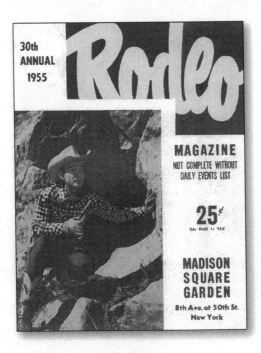

Wrangler picked Virginia and her lovely black, quilted saddle to be photographed with Roy Rogers. After taking several photos, Virginia got along very well with the famous cowboy. She does not know if these pictures were used in any advertisements, but they are treasured. Roy also liked working with Virginia, and the famous cowboy also took a shine to Mat. They were surprised to find they used the same trick caring for their costumes. Hotels had lots of hot water, so the performers often hung their costumes in the bathroom and "steamed" the wrinkles out!

Performing in different arenas called for alterations in the tricks. In this Cossack Drag, the horse was approaching a curved part of the arena. Virginia was on the inside of the curve so she raised her hands to keep them from dragging in the dirt. Here you can clearly see the tennis type shoes she word to trick ride. The ankle high canvas with thin, flexible sole shoes were much better than western boots. She had several pair in different colors.

The costume she is wearing is a combination of a tight shirt over a unique invention of Virginia's: blousy, satin sleeves attached to just a strap which fitted around her bodice. The sleeveless top pulled over the sleeves, leaving them exposed and free. She says this made the outfits versatile, as well as simplifying her laundry tasks since the sleeves rarely got dirty. She was meticulous with her sewing, carrying a portable machine with her almost everywhere, and finishing seams with bias tape. Another trick rider gave her an outfit she had made but outgrew after a pregnancy. When Virginia put it on, the unfinished, ragged seams inside nearly drove her crazy and she was never able to wear the costume in public.

Though she trained in acrobatics and even, at times, traded places with the trapeze artists who would fly above the crowd doing their death defying acts during breaks in the action, Virginia could not gain the flexibility in her legs and hips she wanted.. Her legs just wouldn't go that way. Even when looking at this photo now, she laments, "I never could do the splits."

In 1955, Panhandle Slim hired Virginia as a model. The tailored suit was a pale turquois color accented with black stitching and was altered to fit her small frame. Virginia's image was seen in many advertisements and posters.

She was photographed in this same outfit at the Louisville, Kentucky rodeo on a weekend designated for changing from Standard Time, to Daylight Saving Time. The loss of the hour overnight severely affected the performers' schedules and they felt disheartened, hoping the low mood wouldn't show in their performances.

Also in 1955, Virginia tried doing rope tricks in a dress. This proved problematic and though she was ahead of her time in a mini-skit and fringe, she much preferred the close fitting shorts and two layers of dancers tights she wore with the other outfit. She felt rather naked in the dress, wearing no hose at all. But she could sure high kick and not trip over the rope!

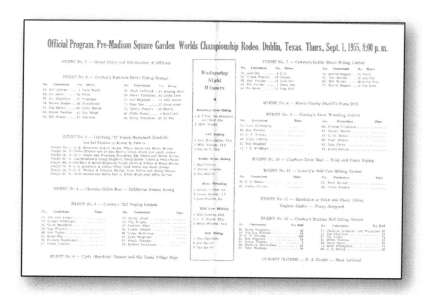

Nancy Kelley Sheppard had worked for Everett Colburn since she was a child. In 1955, he teamed Virginia and Nancy together to create a glamorous two girl trick riding and roping act. They worked well together and performed often as a duo. Often they would coordinate their outfits to appear similar but be in different colors. This created a dramatic appearance.

This is one of Virginia's most famous and favorite promotional photo. She wears the costume designed with Nancy Sheppard, and also, surprisingly, a hairpiece to have more length. Being a mother often causes women to cut their hair and Virginia was no different. But for performing and photographs, she wanted curls to be seen from under her hat.

All usually went well, except one evening when riding in the quadrille. One lady rider did not stay in formation and her horse collided with Virginia's. Down she went into the dirt. The first thing she did was reach up to feel if her hairpiece had fallen off in the tumble. Cowboys hurrying to her laughed at the sight of her not caring if she was covered in dirt and had a skinned elbow, but was only concerned if her hair had come loose!

On the rodeo train to New York City with Colburn's rodeo company and stock, Virginia talked with others who had been to New York with the rodeo and learned some interesting tidbits. She was advised to take her own glassware and utensils packed in her luggage. Upon arrival at the Belvedere, she was not impressed with the facilities. The eleven story building built in the 1920's had not fared well, and seemed permanently dirty.

Sure enough, many of the performers were invited to the Colburn's room for dinner, BYO dinnerware. A hot plate in a closet being the only means of cooking, spaghetti with sauce was the usual main dish.

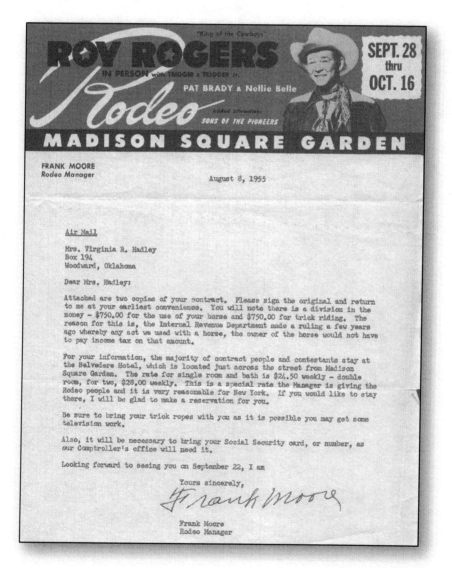

The trick riders were always sent out to do publicity appearances. Here a group is at an appliance store, pretending to make hamburgers in a toaster oven. Nancy Sheppard is in the front left with Virginia by her side.

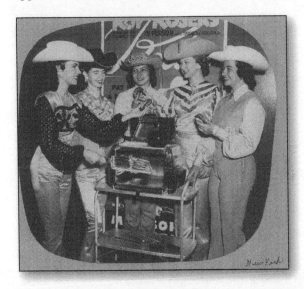

Here is a fine photo of three beauties, Virginia, Nancy, and Joy Sandra, Virginia's favorite trick riding horse.

```
OFFICE MEMORANDUM
MADISON SQUARE GARDEN CORPORATION

TO     Nancy & Virgina          DATE    Oct.11th
FROM   Ken Mac Kay               RE     Television Show.

        For Tomorrow...Wednesday ,Oct.12th.
        Will you please be at 36 West 49th St. at 7:45 A.M. for the
        "Today"  NBC-TV  TV show starring Dave Garaway the show starts at 7:55 A.M
        Bring your ropes and tell them they are made of Irish material.
        also tell them about the 10A.M. Sat.show.
        See. Helen Petretti.....

                                Thank you,
                                           Ken.
```

Virginia and Nancy went to the "Today" studios at NBC per the above instructions. On the set, Virginia made friends with the cameramen and crew before sitting down to visit with Dave Garaway. She immediately disliked the "star" of the show due to his condescending attitude toward people on the set. He would "signal" the cameraman to point the lens at him if he thought it was focused too long on his guest.

She brought two ropes to the set and placed one on the couch next to where she was sitting. Twirling one for a bit, she reached down to pick up the second rope but it wasn't where she left it. Turning, she saw Garaway had picked it up and tied into a bow around his neck. It was all she could to do contain her fury at the disruption of her act, and the kinks put into the rope ruined it. When asked about the statement in the memo of "tell them they are made of Irish material," Virginia says Ken MacKay made that up. One can guess this was done to appeal to the New Yorkers of Irish descent. But she couldn't, it wasn't true.

On another morning show, Virginia made quite an impression. This great letter from the producer of "The Morning Show" expressed his thanks. Virginia doesn't remember this appearance, but it is possible Dick Van Dyke was the anchor when she was there. Of course, he wasn't a famous actor yet and perhaps didn't actually see Virginia. But the producer was happy!

CBS TELEVISION

A Division of Columbia Broadcasting System, Inc

485 MADISON AVENUE, NEW YORK 22, NEW YORK · PLAZA 1-2345

October 24, 1955

Miss Virginia Hadley
c/o Mr. Ken McKay
Madison Square Garden
New York, New York

Dear Miss Hadley:

Just a note to let you know how much we appreciate your coming to our morning show. Your appearance was very well received by our television audience.

We are also doubly grateful because of the early hour rising that was required of you to make our show. This, we know only too well, is a sublime sacrifice to a warm bed at such an early hour of the morning. Therefore, many extra thanks!

Cordially yours,

Charlie Andrews,
Producer

CA/jp

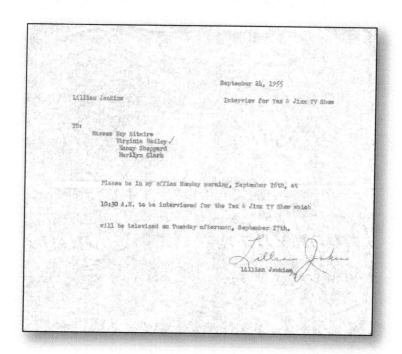

Tex and Jinx were radio and TV legends who originated the "talk show" format in both genres. She was a model and considered one of the most beautiful women of the era—one of the first "supermodels." Charismatic and personable, the pair made a great team. Virginia remembers her as being very nice. They would visit people in their homes to interview, but this time the setting was Lillian's office.

Jinx Falkenburg and Tex McCrary. She was featured on magazine covers over 200 times. Their radio career started with a show called "Hi Jinx."

The proud mama and her little, trick riding son, Mat. This is another photograph staged by Wrangler but likely not ever used.

This is television's Annie Oakley, Gail Davis, often appeared at the rodeos accompanying Gene Autry. Virginia remembers her being a very nice person, but under Autry's control, which did make Gail a star. However, Mat didn't seem very impressed! The photo was taken in Shreveport, Louisiana.

The Cows Love Her Perfume...

By Morris Goldberg

Before Virginia Hadley, America's No. 1 female trick rider, ventures forth on the range on her 1,000-acre Oklahoma ranch to rope a sick calf or mend a fence, she always makes sure that her lipstick is on straight, and that she's wearing a dash of perfume.

"So I'll be feminine," says the glamorous cowgirl.

Doesn't really need to work at it that hard, though. Could omit the lipstick and the perfume and still charm the cows and the cowmen to a standstill.

Copper-red hair down to her shoulders. Hazel eyes. A 34-25-35 figure. Nice!

Makes it a little difficult walking down the street in New York, however. Most other cities, too. Everybody stares. Men. Women. Children. All for different reasons, of course.

Virginia is here for the World Championship Rodeo at Madison Square Garden. When she strolls down the avenue — it's usually Fifth Ave. — she wears a form-fitting Western dress suit of turquoise blue, including trousers, a black string tie, a black beaver sombrero trimmed with rhinestones, and size 7 white boots.

Then the whistling begins.

"Get a horse," the Manhattan Bronx, Brooklyn, and other borough buckeroos shout. Also, "where'd you get them pants?"

The women's eyes grow catty, the children scream, "mama, mama, there's a cowgirl," and the grown-up men just look, and look, and look.

Once in a while a stranger will walk up and take her by the arm, she told me.

But knighthood flowers in the asphalt jungle, and chivalry is not yet dead on Fifth Ave. Because whenever that happens, Virginia said, a big city gallant is sure to gallop up, seize the intruder, and inquire: "This jerk ain't botherin' you none, is he, lady?"

Others will stop her because they want to talk—really talk. Out of the great yearning of the city-bred yokel for the great open spaces, they ask these questions:

Isn't it true that air is so fresh out in the open spaces that it's hard on people to breathe all that clean air if they aren't used to it?

Do the Indians get wild sometimes and run off the reservation?

How early do you have to get up in the morning?

But then life has always been interesting for Virginia. For instance, her romance with her husband, Tom Hadley, a rodeo steer buster and master of ceremonies, is strictly for the story books.

She met him after driving 600 miles through the night from Louisiana to a rodeo in Texas, where he was the MC.

"I had a million things to do," said Virginia, "and he didn't know that I had traveled all night without anybody except my horse. So when I tried to tell him a few things about myself so that he could announce me, he didn't seem to listen, and I got mad."

That night Virginia appeared in the arena under a black spotlight, which picked up her sombrero, riding boots, and her whirling lariat, but left her face invisible.

Tom then and there fell in love with a girl he couldn't see.

"You sure can work that rope," he told her after the show.

After the three-day rodeo was over, they went their separate ways. Then, a month later, Virginia arrived in Hobbs, N. M., and discovered that Tom was the master of ceremonies there.

"Let's go to the movies," Tom said, and not having any thing better to do, I agreed.

"About the second reel of the picture, Tom said, 'we ought to get married.'

"Well, I didn't say anything just then, but as we were leaving the theatre, I told Tom, 'I've been thinking it over and I think you're right.'

"Up until then he hadn't kissed me, but he did when he took me home. It wasn't until three months and two rodeos later that we got married, and Tom was so busy wrestling steers in the meantime that I think he had his arms around those steers more often than he had them around me before we saw the preacher."

Virginia makes about $20,000 a year as a trick rider. But the way she makes it is not for the average housewife or career girl.

One of her stunts is called the Russian drag. With her foot in a high stirrup, she flings herself from the saddle and hangs toward the ground, her hands bouncing in the dirt with the horse at full gallop.

She also does a head stand on her racing Palomino, her shoulders on the horse's neck as she holds on to the saddle horn.

At one rodeo, her horse and that ridden by another girl collided at full gallop, and Virginia rolled completely over the girl's head, knocking her unconscious. There have been other accidents. But her husband has never

Daredevil Cowgirl Does Rodeo Stunts Men Would Shun... But She NEVER FORGETS SHE'S A WOMAN!

RODEO STUNT RIDER Virginia Hadley wears pants on the job... but she doesn't neglect her lipstick..., "so I'll be feminine."

tried to persuade her to give it all up. Thinks women SHOULD work.

"He says it helps marriage because it gives the wife an outside interest," Virginia told me.

They own their ranch at Woodward, Okla., jointly with her parents. Her father, Monta Beger, was the first to train steer to do tricks. Her sister, Dixie, was a trick rider, and her brother, Bud, was a rodeo comedian, but both have now retired.

An uncle, Ike Rude, was the world's champion steer roper for five consecutive years, and her grandfather, W. G. Crouch, provided the first bucking stock for rodeos, she said.

"Woodward is kind of in the tornado country," she explained. "Big winds come over and pick up little things like the small buildings and the fences, mostly, but we like it."

Virginia and Tom have a little, three-year-old cowboy for a son named Mat whose hero is Casey Tibbs, world's top money-winning cowboy, who is with the Madison Square Garden rodeo.

Mat has named his Shetland pony after Casey, Virginia regards as a superior blend of Roy Rogers and Superman. The only toys he owns are 50 horses and bulls, and some miniature cowboy figures. He has never asked for nor wanted any others.

Virginia's schedule on the ranch is enough to make a city slicker shudder. She gets up at five in the morning, prepares breakfast, goes riding with Mat, busies herself three or four hours a day with ranch chores, keeps herself limber on a trapeze, and practices her riding and roping tricks.

She likes to get into dresses whenever she can, to sew, and to cook, and regrets that she can't find the chance to wear high heels often enough.

"I've had to compromise on interior decorations with my husband, who likes things rough," she said. "I get a chance to express myself in my dressing room where I have lots of nylon ruffles, lavender and purple skirts on my dressing table, and purple satin drapes."

Virginia met Marilyn Monroe when she appeared in radio scenes in Marilyn's picture, "Bus Stop," and confided in me this bit of Monroe legend: Marilyn doesn't think she can wear riding pants with her figure.

"She is so terribly wrong," I shouted, and then Virginia reminded me that she had a beauty parlor appointment.

I walked her down Eighth Ave. Everybody stared. Men. Women. Children. But for different reasons, of course.

Then the whistling began.

NEW YORK ENQUIRER

1956

While in New York, Virginia was interviewed by the New York Enquirer, then a respected entertainment newspaper. The reporter wanted to talk in Virginia's hotel room, but she was hesitant at first. But then decided she might not get another opportunity so she agreed. Virginia, and Everett Colburn, were very pleased with the article, it celebrates not only her great looks and style, but skill and prowess as a trick riding performer. Such a high profile newspaper feature proved Virginia's worth with regard to both publicity and performance and everyone chose to overlook the author calling her hat a "sombrero."

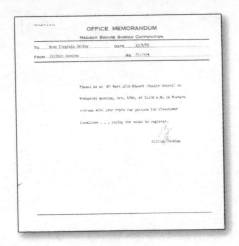

After she arrived in New York City, Virginia received assignments to do appearances at different places, doing different things. This memo from Lillian Jenkins, the person who directed publicity for the Madison Square Garden Rodeo, instructs her to be at 328 W. 48th Street in costume and with rope in hand to "rope the voter to register" for the Eisenhower Committee. In his second term as president, Dwight D. Eisenhower was effective and popular.

Mary Ann Harmes (Fincher) joined Virginia in this publicity stunt. She dropped the rope loop over the man's head. But Virginia literally roped the other man by throwing the loop around him from the back of the horse. He was quite surprised and this may explain the delighted look on Virginia's face!

Virginia, Mary Ann, and a few other ladies were sent to Yonkers Raceway to pose with one of the race horses. The article hit the newspapers with the title "Champs Meet The Champ." The horse named "Adios Harry" was a world champion "pacer." The article did mention the "girls" were scheduled to start at the "Garden" on October 1. The setup for the above was the ladies were to pretend Adios Harry was secretly telling them who would win the race. With the proud bearing of that Thoroughbred, there would be no question in his mind who would win!

The 1955 Madison Square Garden rodeo crew on the steps of a New York City landmark. Note the men in the background wearing overcoats. But not the cowgirls. In fact, Virginia didn't even bring a coat to this photo shoot. The temperature was quite cold and most of the ladies wore their own coats. But Everett Colburn would have none of that. He wanted their fancy clothing to show in the pictures. So off came the ladies' overcoats.

By the time this was taken, the girls around Virginia were shivering and their teeth were chattering. But not Virginia. She was toasty warm. She wore gloves and her parade clothes were a size larger than her usual outfits so she could wear layers. In fact, in this photo, the young woman has on both top and bottom long underwear!

What did Virginia say about wearing long johns in this photo? "Well, it wasn't my first parade!"

This staged shot in 1955 shows how Virginia always managed to get in front of the group. Usually the photographer wanted the ladies in the same order so they didn't have to keep up with each woman's name.

The ironic part of this photograph taken with a United Airlines plane is the fact all the girls on the stairway didn't get to New York City on an airplane. They rode on the rodeo train all the way from Dublin, Texas!

It was not uncommon for the celebrities to take Virginia along on photo shoots and public appearances. Her experience and glamor added to any such event. On this day in 1955, Roy Rogers had her accompany him to a children's hospital in Boston, MA. There a little girl stricken with polio was wheeled out to meet the famous cowboy. As he and Virginia knelt to speak to the girl, each noticed the cart she was in was in terrible disrepair. Peeling paint, poor construction, and splinters ready to snag tender skin testified to the conditions the child endured.

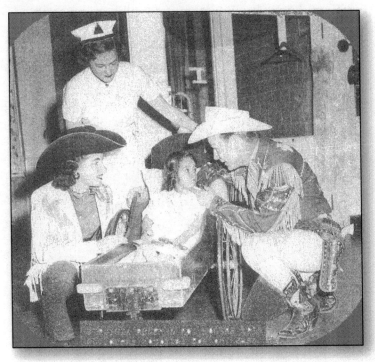

After a few photos, the child was taken away. A very angry Roy then emerged, demanding to see the hospital administrator. The scene was uncomfortable, but ended with Roy Rogers, showing extreme displeasure, handing the administrator a handful of money with the demand each wagon be sanded and painted—one pink and one blue. He promised to return the next day to check the state of the little wagons.

Virginia didn't go the next day to the hospital, but later heard the wagons were indeed painted neatly pink and blue and the staff was contrite. That moment enforced something she already knew. Strength of character and confidence can get things done.

After Virginia and Nancy teamed up as a roping act, they decided to design costumes alike over the winter break in the rodeo season. But with Virginia in Oklahoma and Nancy in Arizona, logistics were an issue. The women wrote letters back and forth describing what they wanted, came to compromises and sewed the costumes independent of each other. When they met up, the matching outfits worked perfectly. And all the work was done by mail and experience.

All of Virginia's life she heard about the Salinas, CA rodeo. Performing at that esteemed event secured one's position as a top trick rider. The clout of having been at Salinas would bring more jobs. When she got the letters below, she knew she had "made it to the top." They even took a publicity photo of her signing the contract!

July 19-22, 1956

While there in California, Opal called from Oklahoma to get a message to her daughter. She said to call home, but it wasn't an emergency. Virginia got that phone message and waited until she was in the hotel room to call. Opal was very excited, stammering over words and having a difficult time speaking. "I thought it wasn't an emergency?" Virginia was concerned. At last Opal relayed the information that an air mail letter had come from the World's Championship Rodeo in New York City. Virginia advised her to open it and read it over the phone.

It was a different sort of offer. There would be no trick riding that year, but they wanted her to do publicity for the event. The pay was good, and the chance to get more publicity for herself was irresistible. After the Salinas rodeo closed, Virginia flew on a jet to New York. She reasoned she had done a good job the year before and gained Lillian Jenkins' respect. Other girls argued and were uncooperative, but not Virginia. She got to the office early to watch and listen to learn what she could from the stern but efficient woman. Virginia was almost thirty years old and still watching for opportunities to learn.

During the performances, Virginia was featured between two male trick riders. They were quite upset at that, as the first act to enter the arena was considered the lowest. But that's how the manager wanted it. Those men wouldn't even speak to Virginia during that show.

Here is another seemingly spontaneous scene which was carefully staged. Nancy wasn't happy being told to put her foot on the trailer tire. The horse Virginia is standing by was only briefly used for trick riding. She says, "He ran funny." In another photo his front legs seem to be quite straight making his stride uncomfortable. Needless to say, that horse was promptly sold.

Jasbo Fulkerson pioneered rodeo clowning. He and his trained mule did all sorts of antics. Once he tried to use a monkey in his act. While waiting to enter the arena for her trick roping act, Virginia felt someone grab her leg. Thinking it was some smart aleck cowboy, she quickly turned and struck out with both of her ropes, landing blows on whatever was there. After realizing the monkey was the culprit, Virginia was surprised to find she had decked Jasbo. But it worked, the monkey did let go of her leg!

At 7, Virginia Hadley Made Her Rodeo Debut

VIRGINIA HADLEY, of Woodward, Okla., the glamorous red-headed trick rider, making her second appearance in Madison Square Garden, started her professional rodeo debut in Cleveland when she was only 7 years old.

She saw the Garden for the first time when she was 5, accompanying her dad who presented the first trained Longhorn steer act, jumping it over an automobile and driving it in front of a buggy. Even then little Virginia had eyes only for the daring trick riders and she vowed that someday she'd appear in New York as a trick rider. The rodeo circuit became her only home.

Her grandfather produced one of the oldest and largest rodeos in Oklahoma; two uncles were contestants and one of them, Ike Rude, was several times world champion steer wrestler. A brother was a top bull rider and a sister was once the nation's best cowgirl calf roper.

Miss Hadley breeds quarter horses and one of them "Joey" set records on short tracks as a three year old. She owns the only silver-laced black saddle in trick riding, and was the first to introduce black light trick roping to rodeo in 1951. Earlier this year she purchased a dude ranch to which she'll devote all her time when she retires from the arena.

Despite the time-consuming duties of her occupation she managed to crowd in a formal education that included a high school diploma and college degree. She also owns a herd of Palomino mares and a saddle factory in northwest Oklahoma.

Miss Hadley stands 5-4, weighs 102 pounds.

The 1956 Worlds Championship Rodeo at Madison Square Garden program features Virginia as a glamorous red-headed trick rider. The quick background cements her status in the rodeo world at the time. She was the only female trick rider that year, and was presented in the center of all the riders.

At Colburn's request, Virginia took an airplane from Louisville, Kentucky to New York City and arrived six days early to work for the publicity office. Her horse had to ride on the train, but arrived in time for her performances which were scheduled for three times daily for twenty-eight days!

At each rodeo, many performers, riders, and sponsor girls were assigned to ride in the quadrille. This is a choreographed dance upon horseback called much like a square dance. Horses were provided which were used in the quadrille. Ladies were teamed with men and they dressed in the same colors. In this photo the satin blouses range from green to blue to red and gold. Notice the brand on their leather chaps. It is the "Lightning C" of Everett Colburn. It was an honor to work for Colburn, and Virginia considered him an excellent leader.

There in New York City, Virginia was again very busy with publicity appearances. Lillian Jenkins had confidence in her and put her in many different situations. Below a whole troupe of sponsor girls, trick ropers, and other young ladies appeared on a New York street with the only canine television star of the time, Rin Tin Tin.

Virginia always carried out her mission, no matter what strange situation she encountered. Here acting as a telephone operator, was one of the more unusual poses.

The black felt hat with the line of rhinestones was a signature look for Virginia. She is seen wearing it in many photos.

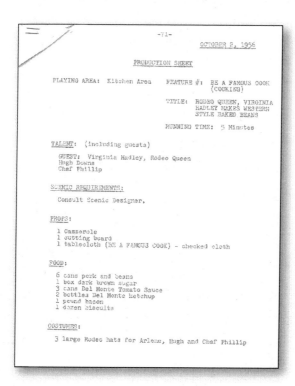

One of the most involved appearances Virginia made in '56 was to appear on the Arlene Frances Show as a celebrity cook. A script was prepared and the five minute scene was carefully planned. Virginia stirred up some western style baked beans, befitting a rodeo gal from Oklahoma. She did straighten them out to not call her a rodeo queen and didn't think the cowboy hats worked so well on the stars. Hugh Downs, the announcer, insisted each time she addressed him to first say his name. She says that seemed a little awkward, but followed instructions and had a very successful appearance.

Again out on the circuit in 1956, Virginia appeared many places across the US. This photo was taken in Phoenix, AZ. An interesting thing happened while she and Mat were there. Filming of a Marilyn Monroe movie was being done and they wanted some western/rodeo type scenes.

The director didn't want actual footage from the rodeo, so after all the regular spectators exited following the show, a whole new batch of people would occupy the stands and arena. It was all staged.

But the director took one look at Mat and wanted him in the movie. So he placed the four year old at the bus stop and instructed him to untuck the western shirt he wore from his jeans and then make a show of tucking it back in. Aghast, Mat refused. An argument ensued with the little boy winning. He said a cowboy doesn't go out in public with his shirt tail hanging out! They never saw the star, the bombshell Marilyn Monroe, but it was exciting just being around the movie people and watching them work.

1957 brought new and different challenges. After working with the World's Championship Rodeo co-owned by Gene Autry and Everett Colburn, Virginia got an offer from Earl Lindsey, Autry's business manager, to appear in Mexico City. He produced a magazine of rodeo contestant statistics which he tried to sell to rodeo cowboys.

Virginia needed to earn some money for a new sewing machine, so she went out and sold subscriptions to that magazine. Her sales effort concentrated on rodeo cowboys saying they should buy it for their mothers and girlfriends back home. That strategy worked!

Virginia came back to Mr. Lyndsey with $200 worth of subscriptions sold. He was so tickled he gave her all the money to get the machine and sponsored her trip to Mexico.

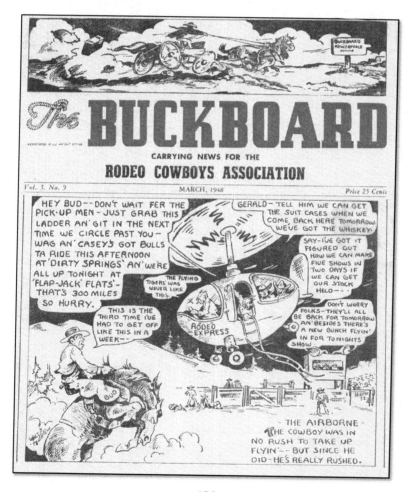

Mat, even at three years old, was learning how to shine in the spotlight. However during one performance, he walked out to join his mom as they had practiced, but something caught his eye. He walked right past her intent on something he could see beyond the pens at the end of the arena. Virginia called to him, and he hurried to her. She knelt down to see if anything was wrong and realized what had mesmerized Mat—a cartoon was showing on the screen at a drive-in theater down the way from the arena.

The above photo taken in Mexico City shows Mat doing the act without a hitch and he was ready to take a bow as the audience applauded. But his timing was off and the spotlight shone in his eyes before he bent over. Quickly turning, he bowed in the other direction, leaving his behind shining toward the President of Mexico.

After the rodeo, Virginia and Mat were presented to the dignitaries. The President seemed irritated and asked the little boy why he turned his back. Mat's honest reply was, "The spotlight was too bright in my eyes." Laughing, the President, dressed in a flamboyant costume himself, picked the boy up and hugged him tightly. Then they were dismissed. But Virginia, always looking for opportunity, got the name of the President's tailor and commissioned an identical suit of clothes for Mat. It was ordered a little on the big side, so he could wear it the next year on the circuit.

The Mexican ropers were the best Virginia ever saw. She said it was like the ropes were extensions of their arms and hands. And though there was a language barrier, they communicated surprisingly well. She remembers them as courteous and genuinely pleasant people and values their signed photograph.

Virginia rode in a car to Mexico City, but did not bring her horse or saddle. She had to borrow a horse to trick ride. After a few training sessions they worked reasonably well together. The saddle was similar to hers at home, but still in the white color popular several years before in the US.

As was always the case, riders were assigned horses in the quadrille. Making this move proved problematic, causing the riders to stretch far to maintain their grip. Virginia reports she did not fall during this session, the cowboy must have eventually let her go.

Also in 1957, Virginia went with the rodeo company to Havana, Cuba. This article saved from a Cuban newspaper states how Gene Autry, the famous singing cowboy and his horse Champion would appear in the rodeo at the "fabuloso" newly constructed Ciudad Deportiva Coliseum.

When the group went into Ciudad Deportiva Coliseum, they were surprised it was completely round. Accustomed to oblong and straight track type arenas, several of the riders asked for an opportunity to practice. They only got thirty minutes which didn't help much at all. Something about riding in a slight curve during the whole act altered the way Virginia and the other riders performed their tricks. It wasn't long before riders were complaining of being "banged up." Virginia's knee swelled to the point she had to rip the inside seam of her pant leg open before it burst or cut off her circulation. The round arena didn't work out so well.

VIRGINIA REGER & son MAT with GENE AUTRY 1957

And here the famous singing cowboy poses with Virginia and Mat near the chutes and gates of the arena. Remember those multi-colored tennis shoes Virginia used for trick riding? Ladies in Cuba went wild over them and wanted to buy each and every pair. So, Virginia sold them all, with the intention of buying more when she got back to the States.

HAVANA, CUBA 5th PERFORMANCE 9:00 P.M.
RODEO JUDGES: BEAL PROCTOR, DALTON, T-A-- & HERB DALTON, DUNCAN, OKLA
RODEO PRODUCER: TOMMY STEINER, AUSTIN, TEXAS
CLOWNS: CHET & BOBBY ----

EVENT NO. 1. OVERTURE
EVENT NO. 2. GRAND ENTRY
EVENT NO. 3. INTRODUCTION OF RODEO OFFICIALS
EVENT NO. 4. NATIONAL ANTHEMS---CUBAN & U. S. A.
EVENT NO. 5. BAREBACK BRONC RIDING

Sidney Johnson	Snyder, Texas	412 Plaza Bar
Clay Lyons	Ft. Davis, Tex	76 Buckwheat
Frank Rhoades	Dallas, Tex	73 Sneaky Pete
Leon Armstrong	Sentinel Butte, N.D.	23 Drug Pot
Bob Burns	Geary, Okla	53 Smart Alec
Chuck Jensen	Blair, Nebr	27 Tootsie Roll
Bob Congors	Del Ray Beach, Fla	321 Honky Tonk

EVENT NO. 6. ...

EVENT NO. 7. JIMMY ADAMS, ROMAN RIDING

EVENT NO. 8. RANCH GIRLS BARREL RACE
Billie Anne Evans, Ft. Davis, Tex   Manuelita Mitchell, Brady
Wanda Rossi   June Ivery, Pampa, Tex
Nerva Dawn Taylor, Dublin, Tex   Wanda Sue Cox, Spicewood, Tex

EVENT NO. 9. REX ROSSI ROPE ACT

EVENT NO. 10. CALF ROPING
Junior Robertson, Waurika, Ok   Dan Taylor, Dublin, Tex
Sidney Johnson, Snyder, Tex   Jym Mitchell, Brady, Tex
Clay Lyons, Ft. Davis, Tex   Tom Hadley, Kerrville, Tex
Morris Patton, Austin, Tex

EVENT NO. 11. GENE AUTRY & CHAMPION & LITTLE CHAMPION

EVENT NO. 12. SADDLE BRONC RIDING
Leon Armstrong   Sentinel Butte, N.D.   331 Joker
Roy Santos   ...   ...
George Williams   Tulsa, Okla   22 Red Belly
Toxic Kidd   Ft. Worth, Tex   130 Pepsi Pete
Alfred Cox   Spicewood, Tex   52 Blue Blazes
Leonard Lanchester   Okla. City, Okla   971 Snuffdipper
Curly Nett   Falls River, Kan   54 Poison Ivy

EVENT NO. 13. REX ROSSI WHIP ACT

EVENT NO. 14. INTERMISSION

EVENT NO. 15. CANNON KAPERS
EVENT NO. 16. BULLDOGGING CONTEST
Charles Morlow, Cleburne, Tex   Buster Davis, Dickens, Tex
Bub Evans, Ft. Davis, Tex   Bernis Johnson, Cleburne, Tex
Bill Ussery, Austin, Tex   Junior Meeks, Cleburne, Tex
Herb Dalton, Duncan, Okla

EVENT NO. 17. DALE ---Y & HIS MELODY RANCH BOYS

EVENT NO. 14. INTERMISSION

EVENT NO. 15. CANNON KAPERS
EVENT NO. 16. BULLDOGGING CONTEST
Charles Morlow, Cleburne, Tex   Buster Davis, Dickens, T
Bub Evans, Ft. Davis, Tex   Bernis Johnson, Cleburne
Bill Ussery, Austin, Tex   Junior Meeks, Cleburne,
Herb Dalton, Duncan, Okla

EVENT NO. 17. DALE ---Y & HIS MELODY RANCH BOYS

EVENT NO. 18. TRICK RIDING
WANDA ROSSI   VIRGINIA HADLEY   JIMMY ADAMS   REX ROSSI

EVENT NO. 19. BULL RIDING CONTEST
Bernis Johnson, Cleburne, Tex   18
Tommy Davis, Network, Okla   16
Jim Bayless, Pueblo, Colo   17
Bub Evans, Ft. Davis, Tex   12
Chuck Jensen, Blair, Nebr   1
Lowell James, Davie, Fla   2

EVENT NO. 20. GRAND FINALE

Virginia models a straw hat with designs for the Moore Hat Company. Straw hats were not well received in rodeo circles being considered very casual and more for the ranch or farm.

But it was just another paying job for Virginia and she didn't mind. Though she would NEVER wear one into the arena or on parade.

A Family on the Road

Since Virginia knew she had to keep in the news to maintain her career, she welcomed any publicity she could get. And since she was pregnant with her second child, Mark, this article kept her legend alive since she wouldn't be performing at the first of the season. Mark was born on 5/9/59 and Virginia again went back on the road with baby in tow only six weeks later.

Making lamps is still a hobby for Virginia. A photo of a recent creation is above, next to the saddle lamp from 1958. Now she unwinds ropes to use the strands as lampshades and places different colors of leather and arrangement of ropes or other embellishments.

When 1959 rolled around, Virginia was again travelling and performing in many rodeos. This beautiful photo was used for publicity.

Mat was doing a trick riding act but insisted on wearing and holding his hat to show he was a boy. When he would sit in the stands to watch the rodeo events, he knew to stay right where he was. Virginia's discipline was that he could not come to the rodeo if he misbehaved. Staying in the hotel with a babysitter was enough incentive to keep Mat in his seat.

Once, while they were working for Tommy Steiner, a top rodeo producer, Mr. Steiner got Virginia's attention and said, "Would you please tell your son it is all right to leave his seat and run an errand for me?" Mat had flatly refused to move. Virginia motioned to him that he could run the errand and he did. Then he promptly returned to his seat. Once when he did wander off, the next rodeo he did stay back at the hotel with the baby sitter. That wasn't going to happen again!

Notice the dark colored saddle. Virginia was in their room gluing fabric to Mat's saddle to dress it up to match his riding outfit. Mark was sleeping in the adjoining room. Suddenly Tommy Steiner burst into room and grabbed Virginia. He rushed her into the hallway telling her to breathe. She felt tired and wanted to lie down. But he kept her walking. The fumes from the glue affected her and it was a lucky thing Steiner noticed it out in the hall. His actions saved the day.

Virginia used photos like this to prove to Mat the audience was watching him closely. Notice their close attention to the little trick rider.

Mat was getting to be a pretty good trick rider at age eight. He would ride into the arena and do tricks like the Cossak Drag, Fender Drag, and Around the Horn. He often rode in the Roman Stand. One evening he was riding past a cowboy who was standing at the edge of the arena. Tricks were done on the straight, and the rider kept to his saddle or stood in the Roman Stand on the curves. Each time Mat rode by, that cowboy flicked his whip at the horse's rump to try to make it run faster.

Virginia waited just outside the arena for her turn to perform. She was to charge in to the arena just as Mat exited. But when he brought the horse to a stop near her, she saw he had tears running down his cheeks. Shocked, she quickly looked for anything obviously wrong, and didn't see blood or torn clothing. The mother instinct caused he to want to run to him, but her horse

knew the cue and took off into the arena. She had to do her act. The show had to go on.

But when she finished her act, Virginia quickly dismounted and passed the reins to a handy cowboy. She hurried to Mat, who was still crying, saying his back hurt. A quick look under his shirt revealed long, red marks.

The cowboy who tried to whip the horse missed and hit the little boy's back. He whipped Mat instead of the horse! That cowboy was mighty apologetic and felt terrible he hurt the little boy. No doubt he was told to keep his whip to himself from then on.

Mat inherited his grandpa Monte's asthma. And travelling so much into different climates and conditions, he would often have breathing issues when they checked into the hotel. In the dry area of Amarillo, Virginia knew steam would help her son, and that the hotels often had a seemingly unlimited supply of hot water. So she would turn on the tub faucet and steam up the bathroom while holding her little son.

Just a week before an episode like this, Virginia freshened the red hair color she was sporting at the time with a henna treatment. Under the steam in the little bathroom, the henna on her hair reacted unexpectedly.

Mat was breathing better, but when Virginia looked in the mirror, her hair was bright orange! Something in the local water caused the henna to morph the hair color to that of a circus clown. Appalled, she began to cry. She was scheduled to be at an event in just a few hours. She could not go with orange hair.

In the hallway, she found a maid who immediately wanted to help the beautiful woman. The maid left the hotel and soon returned with some red hair dye and a friend to help. They quickly repaired the damage and Virginia went out that evening with her usual, lovely red hair.

THE INDIANAPOLIS STAR

Rodeo Is Family Affair

Virginia Hadley is accustomed to finding ropes around her limbs, the skillful trick of her sons, Mat (left) and Mark, the villain this time. The Hadleys frequently have to defend themselves to "nice old ladies" who feel called upon to scold them because the children arrive back at the motel with their parents late at night following the rodeo performances. (Star Photo by Herb Rhodes)

By DONNA SNODGRASS

Mobility is the byword for the Tom Hadley family.

They spend less than a month a year at their ranch near Woodward, Okla. The which starts today in the Indiana State Fair Grandstand.

Tom is announcer for the show. And sometimes his red-haired wife, Virginia,

"I'VE BROUGHT both of the boys along since they were a month old. And I went back to work when each was six weeks old," declares the slender young mother.

"Work" for her is trick-riding and roping in the rodeo.

Before long the Hadleys will be taking the boys back to Oklahoma to launch Mat on what he considers a pretty exciting adventure.

He will enter Ponca Military Academy at Ponca City.

"He can't wait to get into a uniform. He thinks he'll look cute in their cap," says his mother fondly.

THE ONLY thing Mat isn't looking forward to is wearing shoes. His attitude is quite mature, however.

"The only time I wear them is to Sunday School," the tall, slender tow-headed young man comments. "But I suppose boys who wear shoes all the time wouldn't like to wear cowboy boots."

Living from suitcases might be a hardship on some families, but the Hadleys apparently thrive on it.

Each of the boys is allowed to fill a small bag—one he can carry himself—with toys.

THEY DON'T become bored in hotel rooms, are quite self-sufficient and are at ease among adults, be they friends or strangers.

Mrs. Hadley, who is not participating in the show here, makes a point of taking the boys to see whatever there is of interest in each city they visit.

Mat was quite disappointed to learn that the Children's Museum here is closed during August, but his mother promised to take him sometime when they were just passing through.

BEING a hotel homemaker has its advantages, she asserts. "I never have to make a bed . . . I do some of the boys' dozen-shirts-apiece, but not all . . . I don't like grocery shopping anyway . . . Hotel-to-hotel packing is easier than getting ready to leave home, because the hard part is deciding what to take and what not to."

On the debit side, all she mentions is that she likes to bake, but hesitates the first few days at home because she feels out-of-practice and lacks confidence about the outcome.

This article from Indiana speaks of the family's life on the road. It speaks of how the boys could fill a bag they could carry with toys, and how they see the sights of whatever city they visit.

Calling Virginia a "hotel homemaker" is quite accurate and her quote, "I never have to make a bed...I don't like grocery shopping anyway...and hotel to hotel packing is easier than getting ready to leave from home because the hard part is deciding what to take..." She also stated she liked to bake but gets "out of practice" being on the road so much.

The family moved to Kerrville, Texas and Virginia became involved in many events. She helped organize this "Gala Ball" to support the Hill Country Arts Foundation. This photo is from the Kerrville newspaper. A formal affair, an orchestra played for the attendees to dance and a midnight buffet breakfast was served.

Virginia wore a long dress made of gold lame tissue lined with a bright red fabric. It had a very narrow line and was split almost all the way up one side. So what does she do? She wears her trick riding pants under that dress to not feel so "undressed." To look at this photo, one would not suspect there were so many layers covering her small frame!

And remember those painted boots worn in the black light trick roping act? She used them in a Christmas arrangement to hang on their gate and someone stole them! She is still upset about losing those boots.

Virginia participated in many local events and supported her sons in their pursuits.

Mark started showing horses at eight years old. He was very successful in riding and halter classes. Virginia watched him grow in the sport and also helped him to train and learn how to compete in cutting competitions. The boy had horses in his blood and took to training and communicating with the animals naturally. "Excuses Snip" was his pride and joy. They won trophies and ribbons all over Texas. This is Mark at eleven years old.

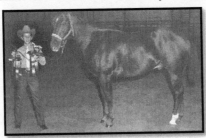

When Mark was about ten, they were at a show and grooming Snip. At home Mark used a step stool to reach the horse's back and mane, but none was available. So Virginia groomed the high side of Snip and Mark handled the low side. During the process Mark would calmly instruct Snip to move this way or that way, and the big horse responded correctly.

Across the aisle a man watched the two work with the horse closely. His scrutiny made Virginia nervous, and she wanted to speak to the man, but refrained for Mark's sake. When they got to the show ring, that man was the judge. With all the information he gathered watching the boy and his horse, he gave Mark the top prize.

Virginia took Mark to a big show in San Antonio, not to show, but to watch. It was a sort of a test, though he didn't know it at the time. She wanted to see how much he knew and his instincts of judging horses. The game was for Mark to pick the winner of each class when they were in the show ring. He studied and chose the entry he believed would win and his pick matched the judges' choices almost every time. Virginia was convinced he was ready for the "big time."

He went on to win world championships in both showing and cutting!

Virginia could make friends with just about anyone. An artist who was an accomplished horseman and loved the rodeo took a liking to Mark and a great friendship was created. Randy Steffen was an artist, sculptor, author, historian, and had a column in "Western Horseman" for many years. He shared tips on saddle and leather repair and other horse related subjects. His sketches became legendary and were made into a book called, "The Horseman's Handbook.". Other books by Steffen were also horse related about historical events such as "The Horse Soldier—1776 - 1943" and "United States Military Saddles—1812—1943."

So when Steffen asked Virginia to help him create a book on trick riding, she jumped at the chance. He took over 100 photos of her in the poses which made up a trick. Holding still in a position was sometimes agony. Usually she just moved and swung her body around. But staying in one place for the photo to be taken proved very difficult. It was tiring and often she was told to do the whole sequence again.

Steffen made notes on the back of the photos, and even drew on them to help create his sketches for the book. There are many hand-written and corresponding typed pages with notes as to what photo/sketch was to be used. Unfortunately, the book was not completed before Steffen's death in 1977. The box containing the photos and manuscript were sent to Virginia. She doesn't know why, and didn't open the box for many years. Mark was with Steffen when he succumbed to congestive heart failure at the young age of fifty-nine.

Here we present some of those photos with Steffen's markings and notes, as well as a sketch he begun, and pages from the hand written manuscript matched with the photos.

Often, Steffen would call Virginia and read some of what he had written to her over the phone. Once when she and Mark were visiting him in his Erath County, Texas home, he asked if she would like to watch him paint. She knew no one was allowed in the studio when he painted and so quickly agreed. Sitting quietly, she watched the painting take form. Steffen was fascinated with Civil War era events and that picture was of a soldier from that time. He knew she would respect his need for concentration and this trust deepened their friendship.

This shows Steffen's attention to detail and how he took the photo and original sketch to represent the movement in a stop action type manner. The project was massive—describing move by move how the rider performed the trick. Of course, Virginia had done these tricks so many times, the movements were natural to her. To see them broken down into individual positions amazing!

The manuscript goes into great detail about the art of trick riding. Only an artist with an eye for shape and movement would be able to capture the flow and beauty of Virginia Reger working her magic.

After the Spotlight

Of course Mat and Mark grew up travelling with their parents. Then Mark got interested in showing horses, which was sometimes at the rodeo and other times at different venues. Virginia found herself over forty years old and felt it was time to retire from performing.

Mark had proved he was serious about horses. After looking at the competition at one show, he announced to his mother that he and Snip could win. A boy competing with veterans. Compete he did, and won that show. He was up and coming in the show and cutting world with his world championships. Mat, however, drifted away from the rodeo life and preferred to stay home and care for the horses.

Meanwhile, the marriage to Tom Hadley deteriorated. But it took two years for Virginia to decide to file for divorce. At that same time, she officially retired from rodeo performing to support Mark with his career. Most rodeo people seemed shocked to hear of the divorce, except one woman.

"No surprise," she said, "the act broke up so the marriage did too. By then Mark had won just about everything he could in Texas. It was time to move back to Oklahoma. Virginia chose Guthrie to make her new start running a Mode O Day ladies' dress shop.

Even though she never worked as a clerk, Virginia knew how to handle people. A natural saleswoman, business was good, but she didn't care for being part of a franchise. They sent standard sets of clothing to all the stores. But tastes in Guthrie were different from those in more urban areas.

Then she met another Mode O Day owner who had a shop in Oklahoma City and wished for more volume of the clothes Virginia couldn't sell. Those items were too modern and even a bit racy for Guthrie. But the other woman claimed she could sell both store's allotment—her clientele was made up of call girls and prostitutes who liked those kinds of clothes. They struck up a deal and transferred clothing under the table, but reported regular sales back to the company.

One customer loved the shop and hinted she might want to buy it. Virginia courted her gently over time until the woman had to have the shop. Mode O Day forbade any owner from making a profit on the sale of the franchise, but Virginia, ever the savvy businesswoman, talked her buyer into giving her $2000 as part of the sale, but that money was not documented. The woman was so happy, she owned the Mode O Day!

Joining the progress of Guthrie is this new and exciting fashion spot introducing these famous labels - Tami - Condor - Scully Leatherwear Jones New York - Chemin de Fer - Jackson Square - Mr. Fine Branch of Joshua Tree
owner
Virginia Reger-Hadley
113 N. 2   282-6774

Unbeknownst to anyone in Guthrie, Virginia was preparing to open another dress shop on her own. On days she travelled to Market Hall in Dallas, Texas to buy merchandise, Opal covered for her saying her daughter was at home sick. When all was ready, an advertisement hit the newspaper announcing "Virginia's of Guthrie" open for business. The sign was put up in the night. She closed the Mode O Day one evening and opened her new shop the next morning. Opal made the elegant drapes using a chiffon type fabric. Virginia worried about hemming all that length, but Opal said it was unnecessary. Indeed, they framed the front door and add an air of sophistication. What an accomplishment!

During the annual "Pioneer Days" celebration in Guthrie, Virginia decided to enter a window decoration contest. Being an independent woman who saw both hardship and prosperity, she designed a display featuring a woman in a graduation cap and gown holding a law degree beside a pioneer woman with laundry on the line, several children, and pregnant with another.  Her window won the contest and several local people were upset that a newcomer received the most votes. The businesswoman who usually won that contest actually "bawled" Virginia out! Of course, that didn't bother Virginia. Her self-confidence and general good nature ignored the woman and enjoyed the win.

Here is Virginia walking the runway as a model around 1979. Rodeo performers from various eras were invited to bring their costumes to the event at what was then the Rodeo Hall of Fame in Oklahoma City, now called the National Cowboy Western Heritage Museum. The outfit she was given to wear was off white with red, ruffled sleeves and red accents. Even in her 50's Virginia cut a stylish figure.

Virginia with her two, grown sons sporting beards and leather jackets.

After a year or so, Monte became very ill. He wanted Virginia to be with him as much as she could. The drive back and forth from Guthrie to Woodward took its toll. She decided to close the dress shop and move back home to help Opal with Monte. It was there Virginia ventured into real estate and bought a house for herself in town.

There were fluffy curtains in the windows which Virginia hated. Opal saw they were of good fabric and said there was just too much length gathered into a small area. The hems bunched and bulged. She promptly took the curtains down and measured. She cut and sewed them into decent drapes. Meanwhile, Virginia saved the material. A few years later, she made this outfit. The skirt and collar are of the curtain fabric. She cut out and glued the llamas onto the skirt. That collar is still in her possession and shown below.. The skirt, sadly, didn't survive the glued appliques and went into the rag pile.

While reading through the newspaper looking for potential real estate leads, Virginia notices a familiar name. Basil Morton had been a classmate in high school and the formal notice stated he and his wife had divorced. Virginia let that sink in for a couple of days, then went to his shoe store, one of eight he owned, and got reacquainted. Sparks immediately flew between the two and he wanted to marry her right away. She resisted, knowing he was just divorced and needed some time. So each of them dated other people and each other for a time. Almost three years passed before she agreed they should marry.

It was small ceremony with little family attending. But this union became an important part of Virginia's life. Basil loved her and she him. They enjoyed each other and had a good marriage. He decided to close his shoe stores and concentrate on Virginia.

Their relationship bloomed and everyone could see the happiness they shared. Basil was very proud of Virginia and was honored to be sharing her life. They stood as an example for young people and were very well known in the area.

Opal and Virginia's Aunt Twila were very supportive of the union. Having also known Basil since he was a young boy.

Before his death in 1983, Monte shared an idea with Virginia and Opal. He though llamas would be the next big thing in ranching. With a growing market for their wool, he thought a herd of llamas would be a good investment. An entire culture was growing with shows, breeding plans, and conventions. The women and Basil decided the time was right. Virginia's new husband had no experience with livestock, but he was willing to learn.

They sold all the horses and Opal planned to finance the first few breeding pairs of llamas. Their money was in an account at the bank which could not be withdrawn without a penalty. Opal arranged to borrow money against that account to get the animals. The Regers had known the banker from the time he was a small child. When she was in high school, Virginia babysat him. Also, a clerk in the bank served as Monte's bookkeeper for many years.

A contract was drawn up and the two bank employees encouraged Opal to sign. Virginia went with her mother and looked at the document. She saw they included the Reger ranch as collateral! A verbal altercation ensued. Virginia grabbed a pen and marked out the section which named the ranch and all its acres as collateral for the loan. Only the money in the timed account was to be listed. Quite a scene it was with old friends betraying old friends. They moved all their accounts to another bank and bought the llamas. Virginia dove in, learning everything she could about the animals. She took a photo of the best llama and traced an outline to use on business cards and appliques like she had done with Bobby's head and her initials in the past.

Basil was a pilot, so he rented a plane to go look at other operations and scout for opportunities to buy and sell the animals. Opal loved riding in the airplane. She insisted on taking binoculars and peered down at the earth below. Of course, they flew over urban areas to get to the rural ranches, and Opal kept looking through the binoculars. Once she spied a man who seemed to be watering a flowerbed near his house. But there was no water hose. She passed the binoculars to Virginia who said, "Opal! You shouldn't be watching a man going to the bathroom in his own back yard!"

Virginia and Basil spent time at each of their houses, but after Monte passed away, Opal asked them to move out to the ranch. She moved into a garage apartment. They expanded the llama herd and Opal loved the animals dearly. Virginia recognized their intelligence and ability to learn, so she and Opal trained them to lead, stand, and even pull a cart, just as Monte had taught Bobby so many years before.

The older woman would often be up early in the morning and go out to pet the llamas. Once Basil was drinking coffee and saw someone out in their pasture. He and Virginia peered into the distance, fearing someone had hopped the fence next to a main road. But it was Opal, out talking and walking with the llamas.

Training the llamas was much like working with horses—one started off small and worked up to the bigger things. Opal felt they were pets. She asked this one to come inside, and it did, just like a dog would. Such training help bring good prices and built strong reputations for the Morton Llamas.

Virginia was often interviewed due to her former celebrity, but she wanted to promote the llama ranch. An article in "News OK" shows how a reporter can blend the two phases of her career. Asked to compare raising llamas to horses, Virginia listed the benefits: no odor, can be housebroken, fences don't have to be as stout, can be kept in a small area, and they don't fight one another. And they're quiet. All except for a hum. A gentle hum from one becomes a symphony of sound from a whole herd!

The trained llamas appeared at nursing homes, parades, stores, schools, and even at Vance Air Force Base. They kept the llamas at the Reger ranch and loved each one of the individual animals.

The Morton llamas were well known around the show circuit.

Basil and this mama and baby won first prize at the Kansas State Fair in 1990. That's a blue ribbon on the side of this picture!.

This is Virginia's favorite photograph she took of a llama. The expression, the wind blowing its hair, and the puffy clouds in the background make for a unique photo.

Always looking for opportunities, Virginia arranged for the veterinary school at Oklahoma State University to use her llamas in their classes, thus receiving inexpensive care and teaching young people about the animals.

Elementary schools heard about the llama ranch and arranged for tours. Always a seamstress, Virginia also learned to crochet and knit. The abundant llama wool presented the chance to learn and demonstrate spinning. This photo is from an event at OSU in Stillwater. Crafts and products made from llama wool were showcased in their area. She truly enjoyed events like this. Getting to talk to people, visit and explain about her own interests was great. Here also is a photo of the little llama toys Virginia made from felted llama wool.

One day in Stillwater, Virginia noticed a young lady walking on a sidewalk. She wore a t-shirt with a barrel racing emblem. Something made Virginia stop to talk to the girl. She hired her on the spot to work with the llamas. The girl was a vet student at OSU and was the best employee they had. She went on to get her veterinary degree and has a practice in North Texas.

Virginia also heard about a book soon to be published called, "Medicine and Surgery of South American Camelids. She talked the school into giving her the author's phone number in California and called Dr. Murray E. Fowler to ask for a copy before it came out. He was quite upset at being bothered, but the charm of the Oklahoma saleswoman won him over and he agreed to send her a pre-release copy for $75. She sent the money gladly. It arrived even before the vet school had one. She used that book often, bought the second edition, and the book is now in its third edition and considered the best veterinary guide for llamas, alpacas, and camels. This is a photo of Virginia's book still in her possession.. She also has the 2nd edition and the book is in it's 3rd.

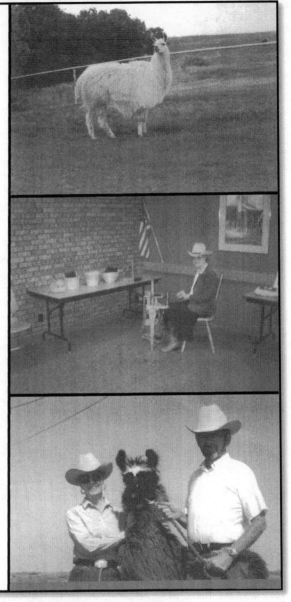

strongly recommend that all new owners join ILA and at least one local association, and subscribe to *Llamas* and as many other publications as they can. We have shown our llamas at Fort Worth, Oklahoma State Fair, Kansas State Fair, Tulsa State Fair and The American Royal.

LLAMAS: What do you feel are the important issues to be discussed about owning llamas?

VIRGINIA: I feel we, as an industry, need to be very cautious in regard to importation. I do understand the need of a broader gene pool, but I'm concerned about the balance in supply and demand. I've never doubted that the prices of our animals would decline from the prices paid at the time we entered the business, and we welcome the opportunity to service more new owners because of it. It does, however, seem that the market stands to be forced to still lower prices because of the added competition. In regard to the larger gene pool, looking at the lack of information on animals' genetic background, it is highly likely that a higher degree of inbreeding cannot be avoided. We also hope there is no rush to shorten the quarantine time for imports. If there is even a slight chance that our existing herd could be in danger it should not be allowed.

LLAMAS: Is this (llamas) how you make your living?

VIRGINIA: We have some other interests, but this is such an enjoyable way to try to do something constructive, it's where we spend most of our energy.

LLAMAS: What is the industry doing in your area and where do you think it is going?

VIRGINIA: We feel it is growing. Maybe because our recent move puts us in an area with more population and better visibility. There are more owners and breeders here in the central part of the state, and we are accessed by more traveled highways. One possible factor is that our people are generally conservative, and now are realizing llamas are going to be around and can be a good and interesting alternative in the livestock business.

We think the industry has a very good chance of being stable and people who are in the business because of a love for the animals will do well. The speculators will probably find something else to get into.

September/October 1994

The Morton Llamas were featured in a 1994 edition of "Llamas—The International Camelid Journal" magazine as shown above. The interviewer kept asking rodeo questions, but Virginia kept her focus. Her purpose for the interview was to promote the llama operation and boost sales.

Indeed, this page features her very intelligent response to a question about importing issues. She said, "I do understand the need of a broader gene pool, but I'm concerned about the balance in supply and demand…" Her business sense was always in the forefront of any endeavor.

A national llama association was in existence, but none was in Oklahoma. Virginia had the idea to pitch a llama show to the state fair committee. Knowing the key was having a contact on or near the committee, she used her rodeo reputation and experience with horse shows to charm an official into recommending the idea to the state fair board.

The proposal was approved, and Virginia put on such a fantastic show it became an annual event. Other stock shows contacted her to have the llamas at their events. She went on to start the Oklahoma Llama Association, knowing it was needed to standardize shows and create a platform on which to build a national presence.

This is an outfit she liked to wear during shows. There was no dress code in 1995, but very soon after one had to be enforced as people were in the arena in flip flops and shorts. Virginia knew to be taken seriously, one had to look serious. Although, she added fun to her clothing in the form of ruffles, lace and llama head appliques.

After Monte's death in 1983, Opal treasured this montage the American Quarter Horse Association, of which Monte had been a director many years, sent to honor the man. Posed here with it on the wall, a photo was to be taken, but she said, "Wait, I need a hat!" Mark quickly removed his and placed it on his grandmother's head.

When Opal's body began failing in the mid-nineties, she and her sister, Twila, were in a nursing home together. Twila's husband, Ace, donated his body to the organ donation program before his death. Twila attended a meeting of people who received organ donations and saw the great positive impact of Ace's donation. She returned to the family fired up about organ donation and had everyone sign up for the program. There was a special protocol for persons who had no heart beat, but remained brain alive for a time. These donors were quickly whisked to surgery. When Opal passed away in 1998, her body went to that program just as Monte's had.

Unfortunately, the Social Security Administration froze her bank accounts. They wanted the monthly benefit returned as it was paid in advance and Opal didn't live for that entire month. Virginia had already used the money to pay bills. It took several weeks, but everything was resolved.

In early 2003, Basil began showing signs of Alzheimer's and life became challenging. He deteriorated to the point Virginia could no longer care for him and decided to send him to a nursing home. His children were against that action, and stated they would care for him in East Texas. She said good-bye to the love of her life that year. He didn't realize what was happening. The man she married sixteen years earlier was no longer in the body she could see. She let him go.

Shortly after, Virginia sold all the llamas and decided to move back to Texas. Mark, now forty-five and on his own, wanted to keep one especially endearing pet llama. They trailered it with all their things to Llano, Texas to make a new life. Mark was very active in team roping and loved raising animals.

One afternoon, he went to Virginia in the house and said their pet llama wouldn't get up. They went into the pasture and he pushed from the rear of the animal. Virginia grasped the halter and pulled from the front. The animal shifted and they could see its intestines were on the ground. Something had ripped its belly open! Sadly, they had to put down their pet. Today, she misses the llamas. Their antics and presence made them a bright spot in her life. The photo below is of one of the prize sires from the herd in Oklahoma.

The move to Llano was a huge change for Virginia. One of the first things she did was go to the public library and introduce herself. The librarian there recognized an opportunity for an upcoming event and invited Virginia to be a speaker. She agreed, and that led to even more speaking engagements.

During that program, Virginia mentioned she was a knitter and had experience with llama wool. Following that talk, a woman walked up to the table where Virginia sat, kicked off a shoe, and plopped her foot up on the table. "I knit, too. I knit socks!" They began talking and Virginia found a group of women who would become close friends.

They met weekly to knit, share projects, heartaches, and triumphs. Anywhere from five to thirty people would gather at a coffee shop called "The Fuel." It was a casual group with no rigid club rules or guidelines. It was just the thing Virginia needed to meet new people.

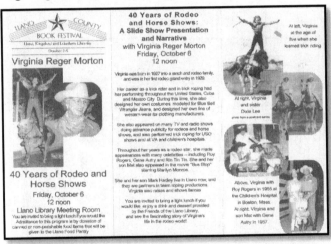

Mark, like Virginia, always looks for opportunities. He saw one in providing roping stock to events. Steers were in high demand and he was happy to provide them. Virginia, as always, helped as much as she could.

Some time in 2006, The Texas Rodeo Cowboy Hall of Fame contacted her to ask if she would like to apply to be inducted. Of course she would, and she sent the information they requested. Her application was accepted and she was included in the group of inductees in 2007.

It was quite an honor to be included in the Texas Rodeo Cowboy Hall of Fame. She received a plaque, a belt buckle, and made many great memories.

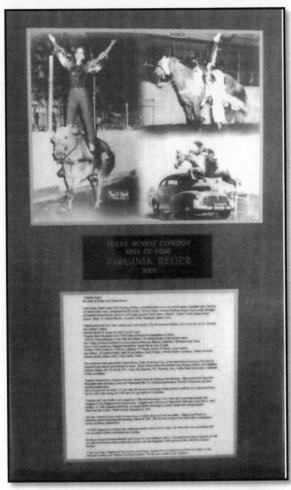

A scrapbook of the event was presented to Virginia and includes pages like this.

Virginia and Mark settled into their new place north of Stephenville. A few neighbors introduced themselves and one was a spinner and knitter. She invited Virginia to a coffee shop across from Tarleton State University called "Beans & Franks."

There Virginia met several other people, including the owner of the restaurant who mentioned she attended OSU. Virginia asked her if she had ever driven past a place outside Stillwater with llamas. Yes, she had! Virginia said, "That was my place." An instant Okie bond occurred and the two women became very close friends.

As always, the older woman helped on the ranch whenever possible. Mark continued his roping productions, so livestock was still a part of everyday life.

When Virginia discovered an antique/art store in Dublin, TX had alpaca wool and yarn, she arranged to go there to check it out. She visited with the owner and even gave her a copy of the jumping over a car photos she carried in her wallet and made sure the woman had her name spelled right—R E G E R—the same forward as backward.

Later that same day, I was in the shop and was told about the woman who came in earlier. The picture was startling. A person on a horse jumping over a car? It seemed unreal. That owner told me Virginia was having a difficult time getting in touch with the Dublin Rodeo Heritage Museum which is focused on Everett Colburn, the Lightning C Ranch, and the Worlds Championship Rodeo. I replied, "Well, I can fix that!" At home, I did what everyone does these days when they want to look something up: I Googled Virginia Reger. Up came a wonderful article written in the Llano paper when she was about to move from that area to Erath County, where I live.

The information in that story washed over me in a wave and I sat right down and wrote a cowboy poem. This is a copy of the one I gave her a few days later. She was at the coffee shop, read it, and looked at me with a tear in her eye saying, "How did you write this without even knowing me?" We bonded right then and there. She had me correct one thing. The line, "That 2000 pounder'd hop over a truck like a deer" started out "...over a truck for a beer." Monte was adamantly against alcohol at the rodeo or around the livestock. Luckily "...like a deer" worked out even better. That poem is on the next page.

Jumpin' Over A Car

She was just a snippet of a girl
But the rodeo producers gave her a whirl
At only eight she'd been ridin' horses for years
So when they gave her a little pony she fell into tears.

From Western Oklahoma, her name is Virginia
Standin' tall in the saddle round and round the arena
She grew up on the circuit back in post World War II
There seemed to be no limit to the tricks she could do.

She'd ride and rope, but the best trick by far
Was when she trained and rode a horse to jump over a car.
Her daddy trained Bobby, a mix breed Long Horn steer
That 2000 pounder'd hop over a truck like a deer.

When she became a woman, Virginia was the star of the show
They'd turn out the spot lights and she'd shore enough glow
With luminosities in her costume, her rope and her boots
And when her cowgirl hat lit up, it was really quite a hoot.

Virginia was always a wonderful sight
Whether ridin' or modelin' those Wranglers so tight
But even she couldn't hardly believe it when
She was booked in New York's Madison Square Garden.

So there was Virginia performing her tricks
With the likes of Roy Rogers, Gene Autry and Tom Mix.
Over the years the rodeo folks knew her name
It was no surprise she made the Texas Rodeo Hall of Fame.

This gal has sixty years of tales of her days on the road
And probably some stories that shouldn't be told.
May we always remember that little gal who went far
Virginia Reger, the cowgirl rodeo star.

A little while later, I was able to arrange for Virginia to meet the Dublin Rodeo people and she toured the museum. They seemed skeptical at first that she was the real thing, but when she found herself in a photograph on their wall, they were convinced she had worked for Colburn. Right away a video interview was arranged and they included her in that year's honor ceremony.

I was with her when she was presented that plaque in 2015. Mary Ann Fincher Harms, who appeared with Virginia in New York City in 1956, was also an honoree. The two were delighted to see each other and have kept in contact. me to write her biography.

Then in 2016, a new display was installed in the Dublin museum.. Large posters were placed high on the walls. Virginia now had her own wall!

There was a cake with pictured of Virginia on it, as shown below. Dean Smith, the famous rodeo cowboy and movie stuntman , was there with his biography. He and Virginia have been friends for many years. Below, right, they look up at her wall.

2016 brought another measure of recognition to Virginia. Stephenville, the Cowboy Capital of Texas, included her in the group of championship cowboys and cowgirl acknowledged by Sundown on the Square..

To keep busy, Virginia creates unique lamps. She unwinds used ropes down to the individual strands and places them one-by-one on shade frames. She decorates the bases with leather, paint, and whatever strikes her. She also knits every day. Notice the llama silhouette on the wall behind the lamp.

Just for fun, Virginia and Mark staged her in a pose just like Opal did back when Virginia was just a small child. An article with Bobby is also in the picture.

And remember that postcard of Virginia and her sister? The artist who introduced Virginia to Elaine created this painting from that postcard.

When asked what impact Virginia has had on their lives, people responded with these comments.

- I met Basil & Virginia through the llama show world as a judge, clinic instructor & exhibitor. The best part of my llama life was meeting the fantastic humans who loved llamas as much as I did! And what a treat to find out she a STAR in the horse world! Basil was so very proud of her & he lit up like a Christmas tree when he talked about her! They were truly delightful couple & I wanted to find the love of my life that I could be that proud of. I did when I found Stan. Thank you Virginia & Basil! - Judy Moser

- Her and her husband taught me what a real hard days work was on their llama ranch in Stillwater. From shoveling manure, feeding and watering, or taking a break with Virginia in the office looking at all the neat stuff she made out of their hair. Spent an afternoon with Basil counting and sorting his massive coin collection as well. Couldn't have asked for nicer people to be around! - A. J. Madden

- I met Virginia later in life, but not only has she become a treasured friend, she's also become an accidental mentor to me. From hearing her stories, I've garnered a lot of wisdom. My favorites are: Observe what is attainable. Decide your preferences in life. Work hard and stick to your highest standards. Share your knowledge. And, never give up.- Pam Patterson

- Besides being lovely and talented, Virginia has proven that it's best to keep on keepin' on.. - Teresa Mayfield

- When I started to rodeo at age 9, competing against pros- Virginia, Tom & their boys were always so sweet & nice to me & letting me help sometimes with their acts! Lots of great memories! - Tina Hodge

- I learned so much from them! She was like a grandmother to me and definitely gave me a home away from home. She is one of the most amazing women I have ever known! I was in awe of her and the rodeo history! I had the best time working for them. Felt like I should have been paying them instead of them paying me! - Jennifer Ennis-Lee

Author's Notes

To say Virginia has impacted my life is an understatement. She has been like a mother, a sister, a friend, and the love I feel for her is mixed up in all those roles. Her story of determination and character should be known, and how a woman can live the life she chooses is a lesson all girls should learn.

This story is not finished. Even as this manuscript goes to be printed, Virginia and I are planning travels and appearances together. She and I will see more people and touch them with her story. I look forward to those times and will treasure the memories.

The process to complete this book has been long and sometimes arduous. Frustration from Virginia that she cannot do what she used to do, and from me trying to manage her mountain of memorabilia. In this digital age, I am glad to be able to preserve her memories for future generations.

Made in the USA
San Bernardino, CA
03 July 2017